THE BOOK OF JOB
A NEW TRANSLATION

THE

BOOK OF JOB

A NEW TRANSLATION

Lee Roy Martin

CPT CPT PRESS
Cleveland, Tennessee

This Book is Dedicated to

REV. CHARLES HARRISON MASON

Founder of the Church of God in Christ
A Man Full of the Spirit of Wisdom

The Book of Job
A New Translation

Published by CPT Press
900 Walker ST NE
Cleveland, TN 37311
USA
email. cptpress@pentecostaltheology.org
website. www.cptpress.com

ISBN-13: 978-1-953358-40-0

Cover art by William Blake – 'Job's Despair' (1825)

TABLE OF CONTENTS

PREFACE

This is a completely new translation of the book of Job, based on the Hebrew text of the *Biblia Hebraica Stuttgartensia*. I offer my deep appreciation for all previous translators of Job, and I acknowledge my indebtedness to them at many points. Although I did not rely on other translations for the exegetical meaning of the text, I sometimes consulted them as I searched for just the right English word that would communicate the meaning of the Hebrew.

I have attempted to produce a translation that is faithful to the original language and that captures its poetic effect. All translation is in part an interpretation, but I have refrained from excessive paraphrasing whenever possible. At some points, this means retaining in the English the ambiguity of the Hebrew. For example, Job 40.24 asks regarding Behemoth, 'Can one take him by his eyes …?' I have translated the verse quite literally, avoiding the temptation to choose one or another interpretation. I have a few explanatory notes at the bottom of the page, and I encourage the reader to consult commentaries on the meaning of ambiguous phrases and idioms. My attempt to stay close to the Hebrew text also means that I have retained the Hebrew personal names for God – 'Yahweh' (יהוה) and 'Shaddai' (שַׁדַּי) – rather than substitute for them the traditional words 'LORD' and 'Almighty'.[a]

As always, I extend my appreciation to Dr. Michael Baker, President of the Pentecostal Theological Seminary,

---

[a] 'Yahweh' is found 32 times in the book of Job, and 'Shaddai' is found 31 times.

and Dr. David S. Han, the Vice President for Academics. They have always encouraged and supported my research and writing for both the church and for the academy.

I currently serve as the James W. Hamilton Professor of Teaching Lay Involvement; therefore, I also extend my gratitude to Jim Hamilton and to his wonderful family, whose vision for lay involvement initiated the faculty chair that provides partial funding for my work.

The support of my family is valuable beyond words. They give me more encouragement and affirmation than anyone deserves. I offer special thanks to my wife Karen for her keen editorial eye and for her willingness to use it to make me look like a skilled writer.

Job is a challenging but powerful book, and I trust that reading it will encourage you to imitate 'the patience of Job' (Jas 5.11) and to worship God for his power and mystery.

Lee Roy Martin
Cleveland, Tennessee
August 12, 2023

ABBREVIATIONS

CEB	Common English Bible
ESV	English Standard Bible
KJV	Authorized King James Version
HALOT	Ludwig Köhler and Walter Baumgartner, *The Hebrew and Aramaic Lexicon of the Old Testament* (2 vols.; Leiden: Brill, Study edn, 2001).
Lit.	Literally
LXX	The Greek translation called the Septuagint. Alfred Rahlfs, *Septuaginta* (Stuttgart: Deutsche Bibelgesellschaft, 1979).
MT	Hebrew Masoretic Text
NASB	New American Standard Bible
NIV	New International Version
NKJV	New King James Version
NLT	New Living Translation
NRSV	New Revised Standard Bible
RSV	Revised Standard Bible
Tyndale	William Tyndale Bible
Wycliffe	Wycliffe Bible

THE BOOK OF JOB
A NEW TRANSLATION

PART I:
JOB IS SEVERELY TESTED (1.1-2.13)

Chapter 1

Job's Character and Wealth

¹ There was a man in the land of Uz whose name was Job; and that man was blameless and upright, and one who feared God and who turned away from evil.ª

² There were born to him seven sons and three daughters.

³ His possessions included seven thousand sheep, three thousand camels, five hundred yoke of oxen, five hundred female donkeys, and very many servants; so that this man

---

ª The book of Job fits into the category of wisdom literature. The Hebrew Bible is divided into three parts: Torah, Prophets, and Writings. Job and other wisdom books are located in the Writings.

The exact location of Uz is unknown, but it is probably north of the Arabian Desert, just west of the Euphrates River. The Bible mentions Uz as a son of Aram (Gen. 10.23), a son of Nahor (Gen. 22.21), and a descendant of Seir (Gen. 36.28).

The phrase 'perfect and upright' does not mean that Job was sinless, but it affirms his integrity and depth of moral character. The description of Job illustrates the blessings of the righteous person as described in Psalm 1. The righteous person of Psalm 1 is Hebrew; but Job was a man of the east (v. 3), which means he probably was not a Hebrew. The name 'Job' may be Arabic, meaning 'to return'. So, Job was a man who always returned to God.

was the greatest of all the people of the east.

⁴ His sons used to go and make a feast in the house of each one on his day, and they would send and call for their three sisters to eat and drink with them.^a

⁵ Now when the days of feasting had run their course, Job sent and sanctified them. He would rise up early in the morning; and he would offer burnt offerings according to the number of them all, because Job said: 'It may be that my sons have sinned, and cursed God in their hearts'. This is what Job would do always.

Attack on Job's Character

⁶ Now there was a day when the sons of God came to present themselves before Yahweh, and Satan also came among them.^b

⁷ And Yahweh said to Satan, 'Where have you come from?' Then Satan answered Yahweh, saying, 'From roaming in the earth, and from walking up and down in it'.

⁸ So Yahweh said to Satan, 'Have you considered my servant Job, that there is none like him on the earth, a blameless and an upright man, one who fears God and turns aside from evil?'

---

^a The form of the Hebrew verbs in vv. 3-4 indicates that the actions of Job and his children were ongoing, repeated events.

^b The 'sons of God' are understood by some interpreters to be *angels* (NIV). The NRSV is less precise, calling them *heavenly beings*. In any case, they are not gods; rather, they are heavenly beings who were created by God and who are lesser than God. The Old Testament mentions several categories of created heavenly beings: angels (Gen. 19.1), cherubim (Gen. 3.24), seraphim (Isa. 6.2), and watchers (Dan. 4.13). The angel of the Lord is a special angel (Gen. 16.7), as is Michael the chief commander (Dan. 10.13; Josh. 5.14).

The Hebrew name *Yahweh* is traditionally translated 'LORD'. It is Israel's covenant name for God as revealed to Moses in Exodus 3. Yahweh is often called the 'I AM'.

The word *Satan* means *accuser* or *adversary*.

⁹ Then Satan answered Yahweh, saying, 'Has Job feared God for nothing?

¹⁰ 'Have you not made a hedge around him, around his household, and around all that he has on every side? You have blessed the work of his hands, and his possessions have increased in the land.

¹¹ 'But stretch out your hand now, and touch all that he has, and he will surely curse you to your face'.

¹² And Yahweh said to Satan, 'Look, all that he has is in your power; only do not stretch out your hand against his person'. So, Satan went out from the presence of Yahweh.ᵃ

Job Loses Property and Children

¹³ Now a day came when his sons and his daughters were eating and drinking wine in their eldest brother's house,

¹⁴ and a messenger came to Job and said, 'The oxen were plowing, and the donkeys were feeding beside them,

¹⁵ 'and the Sabeans attacked themᵇ and took them away; and they killed the servants with the edge of the sword, and only I alone have escaped to tell you'.

¹⁶ While he was still speaking, another came and said, 'The fire of God fell from heaven and burned up the sheep and the servants and consumed them, and I alone have escaped to tell you'.

¹⁷ While he was still speaking, another came and said, 'The Chaldeans formed three companies and made a raid on the camels and have taken them away, and they killed the servants with the edge of the sword, and I alone have escaped to tell you'.

¹⁸ While he was still speaking, another came and said, 'Your sons and your daughters were eating and drinking wine in their eldest brother's house,

---

ᵃ The story of Job demonstrates that Satan's power is limited by God.

ᵇ Lit., *fell on them.*

¹⁹ 'and suddenly a great wind came from across the desert^a and struck the four corners of the house, and it fell on the young people, and they are dead; and I alone have escaped to tell you'.

²⁰ Then Job stood up and tore his robe. And he shaved his head, fell to the ground, and worshiped.

²¹ And he said, 'Naked I came out of my mother's womb, and naked I will return there. Yahweh gave, and Yahweh has taken away; blessed be the name of Yahweh'.

²² In all this, Job did not sin, and he did not accuse God of wrongdoing.

Chapter 2

Job Loses His Health

¹ One day the sons of God came to present themselves before Yahweh, and Satan came also among them to present himself before Yahweh.

² And Yahweh said to Satan, 'Where have you come from?' Then Satan answered Yahweh, saying, 'From roaming in the earth, and from walking up and down in it'.

³ So Yahweh said to Satan, 'Have you considered my servant Job, that there is none like him on the earth, a blameless and an upright man, one who fears God and turns aside from evil? He still holds fast his integrity, although you moved me against him, to destroy him without cause'.

⁴ Then Satan answered Yahweh, saying, 'Skin for skin; yes, all that a man has he will give for his life.

⁵ 'Put forth your hand now and touch his bone and his flesh, and he will curse you to your face'.

---

^a ESV and KJV read *wilderness*.

6 And Yahweh said to Satan, 'Very well, he is in your hand, but spare his life'.

7 Therefore, Satan went out from the presence of Yahweh, and he afflicted Job with severe sores from the sole of his foot to the top of his head.

8 And Job took a piece of broken pottery with which to scrape himself while he was sitting among the ashes.

9 Then his wife said to him, 'Are you still maintaining your integrity? Curse God and die'.

10 But he said to her, 'You speak like one of the foolish women speaks. Will we indeed accept the good from God but not accept the bad?' In all this Job did not sin with his lips.

Job's Three Friends Arrive

11 Three friends of Job heard about all this adversity that had come upon him, and each one came from his own place: Eliphaz the Temanite, Bildad the Shuhite, and Zophar the Naamathite.ᵃ And they agreed together to come to mourn with him and to comfort him.

12 They raised their eyes from a distance, but they did not recognize him, so they raised their voices and wept. Each one tore his robe, and they tossed dust toward heaven on to their heads.ᵇ

ᵃ 'Eliphaz' is an Edomite name (Gen. 36.4), and he was probably from either Teman in Edom, a city known for its wisdom (Jer. 49.7; Obad. 8), or Tema in Arabia. The names 'Bildad' and 'Zophar' are not found elsewhere in the Bible. 'Shuhite' may mean that Bildad was related to Shuah, Abraham's son by Keturah (Gen. 25.2). 'Naamathite' is a mystery, but it may mean that Zophar was from Naamah (Josh. 15.41). Elihu, the fourth friend, will be introduced later (32.1).

ᵇ The tearing of one's robe and the tossing of dust and ashes so that it falls on one's head were signs of deep mourning in the ancient Near East.

13 Then they sat down with him on the ground seven days and seven nights. Meanwhile, no one was speaking to him at all because they saw that his pain was very great.

PART II:
JOB REGRETS THAT HE WAS BORN (3.1-26)

Chapter 3

Job Laments

[1] After this Job opened his mouth[a] and cursed
the day of his birth.

[2] Job said:

[3] 'Let the day perish on which I was born,
and the night in which it was said, "A male child
is conceived".

[4] 'As for that day, let it be darkness;
may God above not regard it,
and may light not shine on it.

[5] 'Let darkness and the shadow of death[b] claim it;
let a cloud dwell on it;
let the blackness of the day terrify it.

[6] 'As for that night, let darkness seize it;
let it not rejoice among the days of the year,
let it not come into the number of the months.

[7] 'Yes, as for that night, let it be barren,

---

[a] It was customary in that day for a suffering person to speak first,
before any visitors offered their words of consolation.

[b] In the ESV and NRSV, *shadow of death* is translated *gloom and deep
darkness.*

let no joyful voice come into it.

8 'Let them curse it who curse the day,
  those who are ready to rouse Leviathan.[a]

9 'Let the stars of its twilight be dark;
  let it look for light, but have none;
  let it not see the flickers[b] of dawn;

10 'because it did not shut the doors of
  my mother's womb,
  nor hide trouble from my eyes.

11 'Why did I not die emerging from the womb?
  Why did I not expire when I came out of the belly?

12 'Why did the knees receive me?
  And why the breasts that I should nurse?

13 'For now I would be lying down and would be quiet,
  I would have slept;
  then I would have rest,

14 'with kings and counsellors of the earth,
  who built ruins for themselves;

15 'or with princes who had gold,
  who filled their houses with silver.

16 'Or would I not be like a discarded miscarriage,
  like infants who never saw light.

17 'There the wicked have stopped causing trouble;
  and there the weary are at rest.

18 'Prisoners are at ease together;
  they do not hear the voice of the oppressor.

19 'The small and great, they are there,
  and the servant is free from his master.

20 'Why is light given to one in misery
  and life to the bitter in soul,

---

[a] Leviathan is usually understood to represent the crocodile. See also
Job 3.8; Ps. 74.14; 104.26; and Isa. 27.1-2.

[b] Literally, *eyelids of the dawn.*

21 'who long for death, but it is not there,
   and they dig for it more than for hidden treasures,
22 'who rejoice exceedingly,
   and are glad when they find the grave?
23 'To a man whose way is hidden,
   and whom God has hedged in?
24 'Because my groaning comes before I eat,[a]
   and my moanings are poured out like water,
25 'because that which terrified me has happened to me,
   and that which I feared has come to me,
26 'I am not at peace, neither am I quiet;
   I do not rest; and trouble has come'.

---

[a] Literally, *my groaning is before my bread.*

PART III:
JOB AND HIS FRIENDS DEBATE THE CAUSE OF SUFFERING (4.1-14.22)

Chapter 4

Eliphaz's First Speech: The Innocent Do Not Suffer

[1] Then Eliphaz the Temanite answered and said,

[2] 'If one attempts a word with you, will you be weary?
   but who can refrain from speaking?

[3] 'Surely you have instructed many,
   and you have strengthened the weak hands.

[4] 'Your words have upheld him who was falling,
   and you have fortified the feeble knees.

[5] 'But now it comes upon you, and you are weary;
   it touches even you, and you are troubled.

[6] 'Is not your fear of God your confidence,
   and the integrity of your ways your hope?

[7] 'Remember now, who being innocent ever perished?
   Or when were the upright ever cut off?

[8] 'Just like I have seen: those who plow iniquity
   and sow trouble, reap the same.

[9] 'By the breath of God they perish,
   and by the blast of his anger they are destroyed.

¹⁰ 'The roaring of the lion,
   and the voice of the fierce lion,
   and the teeth of the young lions are broken.
¹¹ 'The old lion perishes for lack of prey,
   and the cubs of the lioness are scattered.
¹² 'Now a word was brought to me secretly,
   and my ear received a whisper of it.
¹³ 'Amid disquieting thoughts from night visions,
   when deep sleep falls on men,
¹⁴ 'fear and trembling came on me,
   which made all my bones shake.
¹⁵ 'A spirit was passing before my face;
   and the hair on my body was standing up.
¹⁶ 'It stood still, but I could not recognize its appearance;
   a form was in front of my eyes,
   there was silence, and I heard a voice:
¹⁷ "Can a mortal be more righteous than God?
   Can a man be purer than his maker?
¹⁸ "He does not trust in his servants,
   and he charges his angels with error;
¹⁹ "even more, those who dwell in houses of clay,
   whose foundation is in the dust,
   who are crushed before the moth.
²⁰ "From morning to evening they are crushed;
   they perish forever without anyone regarding it.
²¹ "Is not their tent-cord plucked up within them?
   They die, and that without wisdom"'.

Chapter 5

Eliphaz Declares that God Is Just

¹ 'Call out now, is anyone who will answer you?
   And to whom among the holy ones will you turn?

2 'For anger slays the foolish person,
  and jealousy kills the one who is easily deceived.[a]
3 'Yes, I saw the foolish person taking root,
  and quickly I cursed his dwelling.
4 'May his children be far from safety,
  and may they be crushed in the gate without a deliverer;
5 'whose harvest the hungry eat up,
  and take it even out of the thorns,
  and a snare snatches for his wealth.[b]
6 'For affliction does not come forth from the dust,
  nor does trouble sprout up out of the ground;
7 'but humanity is born to trouble,
  as the sparks from a flame rise up to fly away.
8 'Indeed, I myself would seek God,
  and before God I would set forth my case,
9 'he who does the great and the inscrutable,
  wonders without number,
10 'who gives rain on the surface of the ground,
  and sends water on the fields,
11 'setting on high those who are lowly,
  that mourners may be lifted to safety;
12 'frustrating the schemes of the crafty,
  so that their hands cannot perform their plans;
13 'taking the wise in their own craftiness,
  and the counsel of the devious is quickly thwarted.
14 'In the daytime they encounter darkness,
  and at noontime they grope as in the night.
15 'But the needy he saves from the sword of their mouth,
  from the hand of the mighty.

---

[a] Usually translated *simple*, the Hebrew *patah* (פֶּתָה) signifies a person who because of inexperience and/or lack of discernment is easily led astray and deceived. See HALOT.

[b] Meaning uncertain: ESV, *the thirsty pant after his wealth*; NASB, *the schemer is eager for their wealth*.

¹⁶ 'So the helpless one has hope,
and injustice shuts her mouth.

¹⁷ 'O, how happy is the person whom God corrects;
you must not refuse discipline from Shaddai;^a

¹⁸ 'because he bruises, but he applies the bandage;
he wounds, but his hands also heal.

¹⁹ 'In six troubles he will deliver you,
even in seven, no harm will touch you.

²⁰ 'In famine he will redeem you from death:
and in war from the power of the sword.

²¹ 'You will be hidden from the lash of the tongue,
and you will not fear violence when it comes.

²² 'You shall laugh at destruction and famine,
and you shall not fear the beasts of the earth.

²³ 'For you shall have a covenant with the
stones of the field,
and the beasts of the earth shall be at peace with you.

²⁴ 'You shall know that your tent is peaceful,
and you shall inspect your property and find
nothing missing.

²⁵ 'You shall know that your offspring will be many,
and your descendants as the grass of the earth.

²⁶ 'You shall go to the grave in a full age,
as stalks of grain are stacked up in their season.

²⁷ 'Look, we have searched all this, and it is so;
hear it and know it for yourself'.

---

^a Shaddai, which may mean 'Sufficient One', is one of the OT names for God. It is usually translated 'the Almighty'. Job's preference for 'Shaddai' as the name of God supports the view that he was not a Hebrew. Shaddai is found 31 times in the book.

Chapter 6

Job Replies to Eliphaz: My Complaint Is Just

¹ Then Job answered and said,

² 'Oh that my grief was fully weighed,
  and my calamity laid with it on the scales!

³ 'Because now it would be heavier than the
  sand of the sea;
  therefore my words have been rash.

⁴ 'For the arrows of Shaddai are within me;
  my spirit drinks in their poison;
  the terrors of God are arrayed against me.

⁵ 'Does the wild donkey bray when he has grass?
  Or does the ox bellow over his fodder?

⁶ 'Is tasteless food eaten without salt?
  Or is there any taste in the white of an egg?ᵃ

⁷ 'My entire being refuses to touch them;
  they are like loathsome food to me.

⁸ 'O that I might have my request,
  and that God would grant me the thing that I long for!

⁹ 'and that God would be willing to crush me,
  that he would let loose his hand and cut me off!

¹⁰ 'Then I would have comfort;
  I would exult in pain that does not subside,
  because I have not hidden the words of the Holy One.

¹¹ 'What strength do I have, that I should wait?
  And what is my end, that I should prolong my life?

¹² 'Is my strength the strength of stones,
  or is my flesh bronze?

¹³ 'Is it that my help is not within me,
  and that potency is driven from me?

ᵃ Meaning of the Hebrew is uncertain. It may refer to the white of an egg or possibly to the juice of the purslane plant.

¹⁴ 'Anyone who withholds steadfast love from his friend
    forsakes the fear of Shaddai.
¹⁵ 'My brothers have acted deceitfully like a
    seasonal stream,
    like the seasonal torrents that vanish,
¹⁶ 'which are dark because of the ice,
    and into which the snow hides itself.
¹⁷ 'In time they dry up— they vanish!^a
    When it is hot, they disappear from their place.
¹⁸ 'The caravans turn aside from their way;
    they go into the wasteland and perish.
¹⁹ 'The caravans of Tema looked,
    the travelers of Sheba hoped for them.
²⁰ 'They were ashamed because they had trusted;
    they arrived there and were dismayed.
²¹ 'Indeed, now you have become like that;
    you see terror and are afraid.
²² 'Did I say, "Give to me"?
    Or, "From your wealth, bribe me"?
²³ 'Or, "Deliver me from the hand of the adversary"?
    Or, "From the hand of the oppressors, redeem me"?
²⁴ 'Teach me, and I will be silent;
    and make me understand how I have erred.
²⁵ 'How forceful are upright words!
    But what does your arguing prove?
²⁶ 'Do you mean to correct my words?
    And treat my desperate words as wind?
²⁷ 'Yes, you would cast lots for the fatherless,
    and you bargain over your friend.
²⁸ 'And now, please look at me,
    for surely I shall not lie to your face.

---

^a Hebrew lit.: *they are silent.*

²⁹ 'Turn, I pray, let there be no injustice;
　　yes, turn again, my righteousness is in it.ᵃ
³⁰ 'Is there injustice on my tongue?
　　Cannot my taste discern calamity?'

Chapter 7

Job Continues: Life Seems Futile

¹ 'Does not humanity have hard service on earth?
　　Are not their days like the days of a hired laborer?
² 'Like a servant who longs for the shade;
　　and like a hired laborer who looks for his wages,
³ 'so I have been allotted months of futility,
　　and nights of trouble have been appointed to me.
⁴ 'When I lie down, I say,
　　"When shall I arise?"
　　But the night is long, I am full of restlessness
　　until the dawn.
⁵ 'My flesh is clothed with worms and a crust of dust;
　　my skin has hardened and breaks out again.
⁶ 'My days are swifter than a weaver's shuttle
　　and are spent without hope.
⁷ 'Remember that my life is wind;
　　my eye will never again see good.
⁸ 'The eye of him that sees me will behold me no more;
　　your eyes will be on me, but I shall be no more.
⁹ 'As the cloud disappears and vanishes away,
　　so he that goes down to Sheol will come up no more.
¹⁰ 'He will never return to his house,
　　and his place will not recognize him anymore.

ᵃ Taking *righteousness* to mean *vindication*, the NRSV and ESV translate as, *my vindication is at stake.*

¹¹ 'Therefore I will not restrain my mouth;
    I will speak in the anguish of my spirit;
    I will complain in the bitterness of my whole being.
¹² 'Am I the sea, or a sea monster,
    that you set a guard over me?
¹³ 'When I say, "My bed will comfort me,
    my couch will ease my complaint",
¹⁴ 'then you scare me with dreams
    and terrify me with visions,
¹⁵ 'so that my whole being chooses strangling—
    death—rather than my body.[a]
¹⁶ 'I loathe my life! I would not live forever.
    Let me alone, for my days are emptiness.
¹⁷ 'What is man, that you would magnify him,
    and that you should set your heart on him,
¹⁸ 'and that you would attend to him every morning,
    and test him every moment?
¹⁹ 'How long will you not look away from me?
    Will you not let me alone until I swallow my spittle?
²⁰ 'Have I sinned? What am I doing to you,
    you watcher of men?
    Why have you set me as your target, so that
    I am a burden to myself?[b]
²¹ 'And why do you not pardon my transgression,
    and take away my iniquity?
    For now I shall lie down in the dust;
    and you will seek me diligently, but I will not be'.

---

[a] Hebrew lit.: *my bones.*

[b] The LXX reads, *to you* rather than *to myself.*

Chapter 8

Bildad's First Speech: Job Should Repent

1 Then Bildad the Shuhite answered and said,

2 'How long will you speak these things
    and the words of your mouth be like a mighty wind?

3 'Does God pervert judgment?
    Or, does Shaddai pervert justice?

4 'If your children sinned against him,
    he delivered them into the power[a] of their
    transgression.

5 'If you yourself would seek God earnestly
    and seek favor from Shaddai,

6 'if you were pure and upright,
    surely now he would awake himself for you,
    and he would prosper your righteous dwelling.

7 'Though your beginning was small,
    your end would increase greatly.

8 'Please, ask the former generation,
    and consider what their fathers searched out

9 '(for we are but of yesterday and know nothing,
    because our days on earth are a shadow).

10 'Will they not teach you, and tell you,
    and utter words out of their heart?

11 'Can the papyrus grow up without a marsh?
    Can the reed grow without water?

12 'While it is yet green and not cut down,
    it withers before any other plant.

13 'So are the paths of all who forget God,
    and the hope of the godless will perish,

---

[a] Hebrew lit.: *hand*. The hand is often used in the Bible to represent
power and authority.

14 'whose confidence will be cut off,
  and whose trust is a spider's web.[a]
15 'He will lean upon his house, but it will not stand;
  he will hold it fast, but it will not endure.
16 'He is a lush plant before the sun,
  and his branch shoots forth in his garden.
17 'His roots are wrapped around the rock heap,
  and he sees the place of stones.
18 'If he is destroyed from his place,
  then it will deny him, saying, "I have not seen you".
19 'See, this is the joy of his way,
  and out of the earth others will grow.
20 'Surely, God will not cast away a perfect man,
  nor will he strengthen the evildoers.
21 'He will yet fill your mouth with laughter
  and your lips with rejoicing.
22 'Those who hate you will be clothed with shame,
  and the tent of the wicked will be no more'.

Chapter 9

Job Replies to Bildad: There Is No Mediator
1 Then Job answered and said,
2 'Truly, I know it is so,
  but how can a man be just before God?
3 'If one would contend with him,
  he cannot answer him once in a thousand times.
4 'He is wise in heart and mighty in strength—
  who has hardened himself against him and
  prospered?—
5 'he who removes mountains, and they know it not,
  when he overturns them in his anger;

---

[a] Hebrew lit.: *spider's house.*

6 'he who shakes the earth out of its place,
  and its pillars tremble;
7 'he who commands the sun, and it does not rise;
  he seals up the stars;
8 'he who alone spreads out the heavens,
  and treads on the waves of the sea;
9 'he who makes the Bear and Orion,
  Pleiades and the chambers of the south;[a]
10 'he who does great things, beyond discovery,
  yes, and marvelous things beyond number.
11 'Look, he goes by me, and I do not see him;
  he passes on by, but I do not perceive him.
12 'He carries away; who can hinder him?
  Who will say to him, "What are you doing?"
13 'God will not withdraw his anger;
  the helpers of Rahab[b] bow down beneath him.
14 'How, then, can I myself answer him,
  and choose my words to reason with him?
15 'Even if I were righteous I could not answer;
  to my judge I would plead for favor.
16 'If I called and he answered me,
  I would not believe that he had listened to my voice.
17 'For he crushes me with a tempest
  and multiplies my wounds without cause.
18 'He will not allow me to get my breath
  but fills me with bitterness.
19 'If it is a matter of strength— indeed, he is strong!—
  and of justice, who will appoint me a time?

---

[a] Pleiades, Orion, and the Bear are constellations of the stars.
[b] The word *Rahab* means *arrogance*. It is used here and in other Scriptures as a symbol of evil personified (see Ps. 89.11, Isa. 51.9). It can also refer to Egypt (Isa. 30.7; Ps. 87.4).

²⁰ 'Though I were righteous, my own mouth would
condemn me;
though I were perfect, it would prove me perverse.
²¹ 'Though I were perfect, I would not know myself;
I would despise my life.
²² 'It is all one thing. Therefore, I said it,
"He destroys both the perfect and the wicked".
²³ 'If the scourge kills suddenly,
he mocks at the trial of the innocent.
²⁴ 'The earth is given into the hand of the wicked;
he covers the faces of its judges;
if it is not he, then who is it?
²⁵ 'Now my days are swifter than a runner;
they flee away; they see no good.
²⁶ 'They pass by like reed skiffs,
like an eagle that swoops on its prey.
²⁷ 'If I say, "I will forget my complaint;
I will leave off my sad face and be of good cheer",
²⁸ 'I become afraid of all my sorrows;
I know that you will not hold me innocent.
²⁹ 'If I am condemned,
then why do I labor in vain?
³⁰ 'If I wash myself with snow water
and cleanse my hands with soap,
³¹ 'yet you will plunge me into the Pit,^a
and my own clothes will abhor me.
³² 'For he is not a man as I am, that I should answer him,
that we should come together in judgment.
³³ 'There is no mediator between us,
who may lay his hand upon us both.
³⁴ 'Let him take his rod away from me,
and let not dread of him terrify me.

---

^a The 'Pit' refers to the entrance to Sheol.

³⁵ 'Then I would speak and not fear him;
but I am not so in myself.

Chapter 10

Job Despairs of Life
¹ 'My whole being loathes my life;
I will give free expression to my complaint;
I will speak in the bitterness of my whole being.
² 'I will say to God, "Do not condemn me!
Show me why you contend with me.
³ "Does it seem good to you to oppress,
to despise the work of your hands,
and smile on the counsel of the wicked?
⁴ "Do you have eyes of flesh?
Or do you see as a human sees?
⁵ "Are your days like the days of man,
or are your years as the days of a mighty man,
⁶ "that you inquire after my iniquity,
and search after my sin;
⁷ "although you know that I am not wicked;
and there is none who can deliver out of your hand?
⁸ "Your hands have shaped me and fashioned me,
a complete unity, yet you have destroyed me.^a
⁹ "Remember, please, that you fashioned me as clay;
and now will you return me to dust?
¹⁰ "Did you not pour me out like milk,
and curdle me like cheese?
¹¹ "You clothed me with skin and flesh,
and knit me together with bones and sinews.
¹² "You granted me life and steadfast love,
And your care has preserved my spirit.

---

^a Hebrew lit.: *swallowed me.*

¹³ "Yet these things you have hid in your heart;
    I know that this is your decision.ᵃ
¹⁴ "If I sin, then you watch me,
    and you do not acquit me of my iniquity.
¹⁵ "If I am wicked, woe to me;
    and if I am righteous, yet will I not lift up my head;
    I am full of disgrace—look at my affliction!
¹⁶ "And if my head were exalted, you would
    hunt me like a lion,
    and again display your wonders against me.
¹⁷ "You renew your witnesses against me,
    and increase your indignation on me;
    you bring another army against me.
¹⁸ "Why then did you bring me forth from the womb?
    Oh that I had expired, and no eye had seen me,
¹⁹ "as though I had not existed,
    carried from the womb to the grave.
²⁰ "Are not my days few?
    Stop then, and let me alone that I may find a little cheer
²¹ "before I go—and I shall not return—
    even to the land of darkness and the shadow of death,
²² "a land of gloom like blackness,
    the shadow of death without any order,
    and where the light is like blackness".

Chapter 11

Zophar's First Speech: Job Deserves Even Worse
¹ Then Zophar the Naamathite answered and said,
² 'Should a multitude of words be unanswered,
    and should a man full of talk be justified?

ᵃ Hebrew lit.: *this is with you.*

3 'Should your boastings silence others;
   and when you mock, shall no one shame you?
4 'For you say,
      "My teaching is pure,
      and I am clean in your eyes".
5 'But oh, that God would speak
   and open his lips against you,
6 'and that he would show you the secrets of wisdom,
   for prudence has two sides;
   and know that God exacts less of you than your
   iniquity deserves.
7 'Can you find out the deep things of God?
   Can you find out the totality of Shaddai?
8 'It is as high as heaven—what can you do?
   Deeper than Sheol—what can you know?
9 'Its measure is longer than the earth
   and broader than the sea.
10 'If he passes through and shuts up
   and assembles for judgment, who can hinder him?
11 'Because he knows worthless men;
   he sees iniquity also; will he not then consider it?
12 'But an empty-headed man will become intelligent
   when a wild donkey's colt is born a man.
13 'If you prepare your heart
   and stretch out your hands toward him;
14 'if iniquity is in your hand, put it far away;
   and do not let injustice dwell in your tents;
15 'Then you will lift up your face without blemish;
   yes, you will be steadfast and will not fear;
16 'because you will forget misery
   and remember it as waters that passed by.
17 'And your life will be brighter than noonday;
   darkness will be like the morning;

¹⁸ 'and you will trust because there is hope;
  you will look around you and rest in safety.
¹⁹ 'You will lie down, and none will make you afraid;
  and many will plead for your favor.
²⁰ 'But the eyes of the wicked will fail;
  their refuge will be destroyed,
  and their only hope is one last breath'.ᵃ

Chapter 12

Job Rebukes Eliphaz, Bildad, and Zophar

¹ And Job answered and said,
² 'Truly, you are the people,
  and wisdom will die with you!
³ 'But I have understanding as well as you;
  I am not inferior to you.
  Who does not know such things as these?
⁴ 'I am a laughingstock to my neighbor,
  I, who called upon God, and he answered him;
  a righteous, upright man; I am a laughingstock.
⁵ 'In the thought of one who is at ease there is contempt
  for misfortune;
  it is ready for them whose foot slips.
⁶ 'The tents of robbers are at peace,
  and they who provoke God are secure,
  whom God has in his power.ᵇ
⁷ 'But now ask the beasts, and let them teach you;
  and the fowls of the air, let them tell you.
⁸ 'Or complain to the earth, and let it teach you,
  and let the fish of the sea declare to you.

ᵃ The Hebrew says literally, *the exhaling of life.*
ᵇ Hebrew: *in his hand.*

⁹ 'Who among all these does not know
    that the hand of Yahweh has done this?
¹⁰ 'In whose hand is the life of every living thing
    and the breath of all humanity?
¹¹ 'Does not the ear test words
    and the mouth taste its food?
¹² 'Wisdom is with the elderly,
    and understanding comes with long life.
¹³ 'With God are wisdom and strength;
    he has counsel and understanding.
¹⁴ 'Surely, he tears down, and it cannot be rebuilt;
    he shuts someone in, and there can be no release.
¹⁵ 'Surely, he withholds the waters, and they dry up;
    also he sends them out, and they overthrow the earth.
¹⁶ 'With him are strength and wisdom;
    the deceived and the deceiver are his.
¹⁷ 'He leads counselors away stripped
    and makes fools of judges.
¹⁸ 'He has loosened the bonds imposed by kings
    and bound their waist with a belt.
¹⁹ 'He leads away priests stripped
    and overthrows the mighty.
²⁰ 'He removes speech from the trusted ones,
    and takes away the understanding of the aged.
²¹ 'He pours contempt upon princes,
    and loosens the belt of the mighty.
²² 'He uncovers deep things out of darkness,
    and brings the shadow of death to light.
²³ 'He increases the nations and destroys them;
    he enlarges the nations and guides them.
²⁴ 'He takes away the understanding of the chiefs of the
    people of the earth
    and causes them to wander in a wilderness
    where there is no path.

25 'They grope in the dark without light,
   and he makes them to stagger like a drunken man.

Chapter 13

Job Expresses Hope
1 'Look, my eye has seen all this;
   my ear has heard and understood it.
2 'What you know, the same do I know also;
   I am not inferior to you.
3 'Surely I would speak to Shaddai,
   and I desire to reason with God.
4 'But you plaster over with lies;
   you are all worthless physicians.
5 'Oh, that you would altogether hold your peace;
   that would be your wisdom.
6 'Hear now my reasoning,
   and listen to the pleadings of my lips.
7 'Will you speak falsely for God?
   And talk deceitfully for him?
8 'Will you show partiality for him?
   Will you plead for God?
9 'Will it be well for you when he searches you out?
   Or, like one person deceives another,
   can you deceive him?
10 'He will surely rebuke you,
   if you secretly show partiality.
11 'Will not his excellence make you afraid,
   and the dread of him fall upon you?
12 'Your memorable sayings are proverbs of ashes,
   your answers are answers of clay.
13 'Be silent before me, and I will speak,
   and let come on me what may.

14 'Why should I take my flesh in my teeth,
   and put my life in my hand?
15 'Though he slay me, yet will I wait for him;
   but I will defend my ways before him.
16 'This also is my salvation,
   that the godless may not come before him.
17 'Listen carefully to my speech,
   and let my declaration be in your ears.
18 'See now, I have prepared my case;
   I know that I will be vindicated.
19 'Who is there that will contend with me?
   For then I would be silent and breathe my last.
20 'Only two things do not do to me,
   then will I not hide myself from you:
21 'withdraw your hand far from me,
   and let not the dread of you make me afraid.
22 'Then call, and I will answer;
   or let me speak, and you answer me.
23 'How many are my iniquities and sins?
   Make known to me my transgression and my sin.
24 'Why do you hide your face
   and regard me as your enemy?
25 'Will you frighten a windblown leaf;
   and will you chase a dry husk?
26 'For you write bitter things against me
   and make me inherit the iniquities of my youth.
27 'You put my feet in the stocks
   and watch closely all my paths;
   you engrave marks on the souls of my feet.
28 'And, like a rotten thing, one disintegrates,
   like a garment that is moth-eaten.

Chapter 14

Job Explains that Death Comes to All

¹ 'Man, who is born of a woman,
   is of few days and full of trouble.

² 'He comes forth like a flower and withers;
   he flees like a shadow and does not continue.

³ 'Do you open your eyes on such a one,
   and bring me[a] into judgment with you?

⁴ 'Who can bring a clean thing out of an unclean?
   No one!

⁵ 'Seeing his days are determined,
   the number of his months are with you,
   you have appointed his bounds that he cannot pass,

⁶ 'turn from him, that he may rest,
   until he, as a hired man, finishes his day.

⁷ 'For there is hope for a tree,
   if it is cut down, that it will sprout again,
   and that its tender shoots will not cease.

⁸ 'Though its root may grow old in the earth,
   and its stump may die in the ground;

⁹ 'yet at the scent of water it will bud
   and bring forth boughs like a plant.

¹⁰ 'But a man dies and lies prostrate;
   he breathes his last, and where is he?

¹¹ 'As the waters disappear from the sea,
   and a river drains away and dries up,

¹² 'so a human lies down, and does not rise;
   until the heavens are no more
   he will not awake nor be roused out of his sleep.

---

[a] The LXX reads *him* instead of *me*.

¹³ 'Oh, that you would hide me in Sheol,
  that you would conceal me until your wrath is past,
  that you would appoint me a set time
  and remember me!
¹⁴ 'If a man dies, will he live again?
  All the days of my service will I wait,
  until my release comes.
¹⁵ 'You will call, and I will answer you;
  you will long for the work of your hands.
¹⁶ 'But now, you number my steps.
  Do you not observe my sin?
¹⁷ 'My transgression is sealed up in a bag,
  and you cover[a] over my iniquity.
¹⁸ 'Indeed, the mountain falls and withers,
  and the rock is removed from its place.
¹⁹ 'The waters wear away the stones;
  its torrents wash away the dust of the earth;
  and you destroy the hope of man.
²⁰ 'You overpower him forever, and he goes away;
  you change his countenance and send him away.
²¹ 'His sons come to honor, and he does not know it;
  and they are brought low, but he does not perceive it.
²² 'But he feels the pain of his body,
  and his whole being mourns'.

---

[a] The Hebrew states, *you plaster my iniquity.*

PART IV:
JOB AND HIS FRIENDS DISCUSS THE FATE OF THE WICKED (15.1-21.34)

Chapter 15

Eliphaz's Second Speech: Job Does not Fear God

¹ Then Eliphaz the Temanite answered and said,
² 'Should a wise man reply with empty knowledge
    and fill his belly with the east wind?
³ 'Should he argue with useless talk,
    or with speeches with which he can do no good?
⁴ 'Surely, you do away with fear,
    and hinder meditation before God.
⁵ 'Because your iniquity teaches your mouth,
    and you choose the tongue of the crafty;
⁶ 'your own mouth condemns you, and not I;
    yes, your own lips testify against you.
⁷ 'Are you the first man that was born,
    or were you brought forth before the hills?
⁸ 'Have you heard the secret counsel of God;
    and do you restrict wisdom to yourself?
⁹ 'What do you know that we do not know;
    what do you understand that we do not?
¹⁰ 'Both the gray-haired and aged are among us,
    older than your father.

¹¹ 'Are God's comforts too small for you;
   and is a gentle word not enough for you?
¹² 'Why does your heart carry you away,
   and why do your eyes flash
¹³ 'that you turn your spirit against God,
   and let such words go out of your mouth?
¹⁴ 'What is man that he could be pure,
   and he who is born of a woman,
   that he could be righteous?
¹⁵ 'Behold, God puts no trust even in his holy ones;
   and the heavens are not clean in his sight.
¹⁶ 'How much more abhorred and corrupt
   is man who drinks injustice like water!
¹⁷ 'I will show you; hear me;
   and this that I have seen I will declare—
¹⁸ 'what wise men have told,
   not hiding anything received from their fathers,
¹⁹ 'to whom alone the land was given,
   and no foreigner passed among them:
²⁰ 'the wicked man travails with pain all his days,
   and numbered are the years stored up
   for the oppressor.
²¹ 'A dreadful sound is in his ears;
   in prosperity the destroyer will come upon him.
²² 'He does not believe that he will return from darkness,
   and a sword awaits him.
²³ 'He wanders about for bread, saying, 'Where is it?'
   He knows that the day of darkness is ready at his hand.
²⁴ 'Distress and anguish make him afraid;
   they overpower him, like a king ready for battle.
²⁵ 'Because he stretches out his hand against God,
   and strengthens himself against Shaddai,
²⁶ 'he rushes upon him, even on his neck,
   with his thick embossed shield.

27 'Because he has covered his face with his fatness
and gathered fat upon his waist,
28 'he has dwelt in desolate cities
and in houses which no one inhabits,
which are ready to become heaps.
29 'He will not be rich, nor will his wealth continue,
nor will his possessions spread over the earth.
30 'He will never escape the darkness;
the flame will dry out his branches,
and by the breath of his mouth will he go away.
31 'Let not him that is deceived trust in futility,
because futility will be his reward.
32 'It will be accomplished before his time,
and his branch will not be green.
33 'He will shake off his unripe grape like the vine,
and will cast off his blossom like the olive,
34 'because the company of the godless will be desolate,
and fire will consume the tents of bribery.
35 'They conceive mischief, and give birth to futility,
and their womb prepares deceit'.

Chapter 16

Job Replies to Eliphaz's Second Speech
1 Then Job answered and said,
2 'I have heard many such things;
miserable comforters are you all!
3 'Is there an end to windy words,
or what provokes you that you answer?
4 'I also could speak as you do,
If you were in my place.
I could heap up words against you
and shake my head at you.

5 'But I would strengthen you with my mouth,
  and the moving of my lips would relieve your grief.
6 'Though I speak, my grief is not relieved,
  and though I stop, what am I eased?
7 'But now, God has made me weary;
  you have made desolate all my company.
8 'You have filled me with wrinkles,
  which witness against me;
  and my leanness rises up against me
  and testifies to my face.
9 'He has torn me in his wrath,
  and he has carried a grudge against me.
  He has gnashed upon me with his teeth;
  my adversary sharpens his gaze upon me.
10 'They have gaped upon me with their mouth;
  they have struck me upon the cheek reproachfully;
  they have gathered themselves together against me.
11 'God has delivered me to the ungodly,
  and turned me over into the hands of the wicked.
12 'I was at ease, but he shattered me;
  he also has taken me by my neck,
  and shaken me to pieces,
  and set me up for his target.
13 'His archers surround me;
  he splits open my kidneys, and does not pity;
  he pours out my gall upon the ground.
14 'He pierces me with thrust upon thrust;
  he rushes upon me like a warrior.
15 'I have sewn sackcloth over my skin,
  and thrust my horn into the dust.
16 'My face is inflamed with weeping,
  and on my eyelids is the shadow of death;
17 'although there is no violence in my hands,
  and my prayer is pure.

¹⁸ 'O earth, do not cover my blood,
and let my cry have no resting place.
¹⁹ 'Also now, look, my witness is in heaven,
and my record is on high.
²⁰ 'My friends scorn me,
and my eyes pour out tears to God.
²¹ 'Oh, that one might plead for a man with God,
as a man pleads for his neighbor!
²² 'When a few years have come,
then I will go the way from which I will not return.

Chapter 17

Job Seeks Relief

¹ 'My spirit is broken,
my days are extinguished,
the grave is ready for me.
² 'Surely, mockers are with me,
and my eye dwells on their provocation.
³ 'Now put down a pledge for me with yourself.
Who is there that will put up security for me?[a]
⁴ 'Because you have closed their minds from
understanding;
therefore, you will not exalt them.
⁵ 'He who betrays his friends for reward,
the eyes of his children will fail.
⁶ 'He has made me a byword of the people—
someone in whose face they spit.
⁷ 'My eye also has grown dim from sorrow,
and all my members are like a shadow.

---

[a] The Hebrew says, *strike hands with me,* which means to make an agreement, as in signing a contract.

⁸ 'Upright men are astonished at this,
  and the innocent stir themselves against the godless.
⁹ 'Yet the righteous holds to his way,
  and he that has clean hands grows
  stronger and stronger.
¹⁰ 'But as for you^a all, return and come now,
  and I will not find one wise man among you.
¹¹ 'My days are past, my plans are broken off,
  the desires of my heart.
¹² 'They change the night into day;
  the light is short because of darkness.
¹³ 'If I hope for Sheol as my house
  and make my bed in the darkness,
¹⁴ 'if I say to the grave, "You are my father";
  to the worm, "You are my mother and my sister";
¹⁵ 'where then is my hope?
  As for my hope, who will see it?
¹⁶ 'Will it go down to the bars of Sheol?
  Shall we descend together in the dust?'

Chapter 18

Bildad's Second Speech: God Punishes the Wicked
¹ Then Bildad the Shuhite answered and said,
² 'How long will you hunt for words?
  Consider, and afterwards we will speak.
³ 'Why are we counted as cattle
  and regarded as stupid in your sight?
⁴ 'You who tear yourself in anger—
  will the earth be forsaken for you,
  and will the rock be removed from its place?

---

^a The LXX reads, *them.*

5 'Yes, the light of the wicked will be extinguished,
   and the flame of his fire will not shine.
6 'The light is dark in his tent,
   and his lamp beside him will be extinguished.
7 'His strong steps will be shortened,
   and his own schemes will cast him down.
8 'Because he is cast into a net by his own feet,
   and he walks upon a snare,
9 'a trap takes him by the heel,
   and a snare lays hold on him.
10 'A snare is laid for him in the ground,
   and a trap for him in the path.
11 'Terrors frighten him on every side,
   and chase him at his heels.
12 'His strength will be hungry,
   and calamity will be ready at his side.
13 'It will devour the parts of his skin;
   the firstborn of death will devour his limbs.
14 'He is ripped out of his tent in which he trusted,
   and marched off to the king of terrors.
15 'They dwell in his tent who are none of his;
   sulfur is scattered upon his habitation.
16 'His roots will be dried up beneath,
   and above, his branch will cut off.
17 'The memory of him will perish from the earth,
   and he will have no name in the street.
18 'He will be driven from light into darkness
   and chased out of the world.
19 'He has neither descendant nor
   posterity among his people,
   nor any remaining in his dwellings.
20 'They who come after him will be astonished at his day,
   just as they who came before him were
   seized with fright.

21 'Surely such are the dwellings of the unrighteous,
   and this is the place of him who does not know God'.

Chapter 19

Job Replies to Bildad's Second Speech
1 Then Job answered and said,
2 'How long will you torment my whole being
   and break me in pieces with words?
3 'These ten times you have humiliated me;
   are you not ashamed that you wrong me?
4 'And if indeed I have erred,
   my error remains with me.
5 'If indeed you magnify yourselves against me
   and make my disgrace an argument against me,
6 'know now that God has wronged me
   and has surrounded me with his net.
7 'Look, I cry out concerning violence,
   but I am not answered;
   I cry aloud, but there is no justice.
8 'He has fenced up my way that I cannot pass,
   and he has set darkness in my paths.
9 'He has stripped me of my glory,
   and taken the crown from my head.
10 'He has torn me down on every side, and I am gone,
   and my hope he has uprooted like a tree.
11 'He has also kindled his wrath against me,
   and he counts me as one of his enemies.
12 'His troops come together
   and build up their road against me
   and encamp all around my tent.
13 'He has removed my brothers far from me,
   and those who know me are completely
   estranged from me.

¹⁴ 'My relatives have failed,
   and those who know me have forgotten me.
¹⁵ 'Those who dwell in my house and my maidservants,
   consider me a stranger;
   I have become a foreigner in their sight.
¹⁶ 'I call to my servant, but he does not answer;
   with my mouth I plead with him for favor.
¹⁷ 'My breath is offensive to my wife;
   I am loathsome to the children of my own body.
¹⁸ 'Yes, young children despise me;
   when I rise up, they speak against me.
¹⁹ 'All my close friends detest me,
   and they whom I love have turned against me.
²⁰ 'My bones cling to my skin and to my flesh,
   and I have escaped by the skin of my teeth.
²¹ 'Have pity upon me, have pity upon me,
   O you my friends;
   for the hand of God has touched me.
²² 'Why do you, like God, pursue me
   and are not satisfied with my flesh?

Job Declares, My Redeemer Lives

²³ 'Oh, that my words were written!
   Oh, that they were inscribed in a book!
²⁴ 'That with an iron pen and lead
   they were engraved in the rock forever!
²⁵ 'And as for me, I know that my redeemer lives,
   and he will stand at last on the earth.
²⁶ 'And after my skin is destroyed,
   yet in my flesh I shall see God,
²⁷ 'whom I will see for myself,
   and my eyes will behold, and not another;
   how my heart yearns within me.
²⁸ 'If you should say, "How shall we pursue him?",
   and "The root of the matter is found in him";

²⁹ 'be afraid of the sword for yourselves,
  because wrath brings the punishments of the sword,
  that you may know there is judgment'.

Chapter 20

Zophar's Second Speech: The Wicked Suffer

¹ Then Zophar the Naamathite answered and said,

² 'Therefore my thoughts cause me to answer,
  because of my agitation within me.

³ 'I hear the rebuke that disgraces me,
  and a spirit beyond my understanding answers me.

⁴ 'Do you not know this of old,
  since man was placed upon earth,

⁵ 'that the exulting of the wicked is short,
  and the joy of the godless is but for a moment?

⁶ 'Though his loftiness extends to the heavens,
  and his head reaches to the clouds,

⁷ 'yet he will perish forever like his own excrement;
  those who have seen him will say, "Where is he?"

⁸ 'He will fly away like a dream and will not be found;
  yes, he will be chased away as a vision of the night.

⁹ 'The eye that saw him will see him no more,
  nor will his place behold him anymore.

¹⁰ 'His children will seek favor from the poor,
  and his hands will give back his wealth.

¹¹ 'His bones are full of his youthful vigor,
  but it will lie down with him in the dust.

¹² 'Though evil is sweet in his mouth,
  and he hides it under his tongue;

¹³ 'though he spares it and does not forsake it,
  but keeps it in his mouth;

¹⁴ 'yet his food in his stomach turns sour;
  it becomes the venom of cobras within him.

¹⁵ 'He has swallowed down riches,
and he will vomit them up again;
God will cast them out of his belly.
¹⁶ 'He will suck the poison of cobras;
the viper's tongue will slay him.
¹⁷ 'He will not see the streams, the rivers,
the torrents of honey and curds.
¹⁸ 'He will return what he has gained and
will not swallow it down,
like his profit from trade, he will not rejoice in it;
¹⁹ 'because he has oppressed and forsaken the poor;
he has taken by force a house which he did not build.
²⁰ 'Because he knows no quietness in his belly,
he will not retain anything he desired.
²¹ 'Nothing is left for him to eat,
therefore, his prosperity will not endure.
²² 'In his plentiful fullness it will be stressful for him;
every kind of misery[a] will come upon him.
²³ 'While filling his belly, God will send his burning anger,
and will rain it on him while he is eating.
²⁴ 'He will flee from the iron weapon;
a bronze bow will pierce him through.
²⁵ 'It is drawn, and comes out of his body;
and the glittering point from his gall;[b]
terrors come upon him.
²⁶ 'Total darkness is laid up for his treasures;
an unfanned fire will consume him;
it will go ill with him who is left in his tent.
²⁷ 'The heavens will reveal his iniquity,
and the earth will rise up against him.

---

[a] The Hebrew reads, *every hand of misery.*

[b] Lit.: *gallbladder.*

²⁸ 'The possessions of his house will depart,
    flowing away in the day of his wrath.

²⁹ 'This is the wicked man's portion from God,
    and the inheritance promised him from God'.

Chapter 21

Job Replies to Zophar's Second Speech

¹ Then Job answered and said:

² 'Listen carefully to my speech,
    and let this be your comfort.

³ 'Bear with me and I myself will speak,
    and, after I have spoken, mock on.

⁴ 'As for me, is my complaint against another human?
    Why then should I not be impatient?

⁵ 'Look at me and be astonished,
    and put your hand over your mouth.

⁶ 'When I think of it, I am terrified,
    and trembling seizes my flesh.

⁷ 'Why do the wicked live on, reach old age,
    and become mighty in power?

⁸ 'Their descendants are established in their presence,
    and their offspring before their eyes.

⁹ 'Their houses are safe from fear,
    and the rod of God is not upon them.

¹⁰ 'His bull breeds without failure;
    his cow calves without miscarriage.

¹¹ 'They send forth their little ones like a flock,
    and their children dance about.

¹² 'They take up the tambourine and harp
    and rejoice at the sound of the flute.

¹³ 'They finish their days in prosperity,
    then go down peacefully to Sheol.

14 'Therefore they say to God, "Turn aside from us,
   for we do not desire to know your ways.
15 "Who is Shaddai, that we should serve him;
   and what profit do we have if we pray to him?"
16 'Indeed, is not their prosperity in their hand?
   The counsel of the wicked is far from me.
17 'How often is the lamp of the wicked snuffed out,
   that calamity comes upon them,
   that God distributes destruction in his anger?
18 'Are they like straw before the wind
   and like chaff that a storm carries away?
19 'You say that God stores up their iniquity
   for their children;
   Let him reward the people themselves,
   and they will know it.
20 'Let their eyes see their own destruction,
   and let them drink of the wrath of Shaddai.
21 'For what do they care about their
   households after them,
   when the number of their months is cut off?
22 'Can anyone teach God knowledge,
   since he judges those that are on high?
23 'One dies in his full strength,
   being wholly at ease and secure.
24 'His buckets[a] are full of milk,
   and the marrow of his bones is moist.
25 'Another dies in complete bitterness,
   never having tasted happiness.
26 'They will lie down alike in the dust,
   and worms will cover them.
27 'Look, I know your thoughts,
   and the schemes with which you would wrong me.

---

[a] The LXX reads, *bowels.*

²⁸ 'For you say, "Where is the house of the prince,
and where is the tent of the wicked?"

²⁹ 'Have you not asked them that travel the road,
and do you not consider their testimony

³⁰ 'that an evil person is spared in the day of disaster
and are rescued in the day of wrath?

³¹ 'Who declares his way to his face,
and who repays him for what he has done?

³² 'He is brought to the grave,
and a watch is kept over the tomb.

³³ 'The clods of the valley are sweet to him,
and everyone follows him,
and countless go before him.

³⁴ 'How then can you comfort me with emptiness,
with your answers in which remains only falsehood?'

PART V:
JOB RESPONDS TO ACCUSATIONS (22.1-27.23)

Chapter 22

Eliphaz's Third Speech: Job is Wicked

¹ Then Eliphaz the Temanite answered and said,

² 'Can a strong man be of use to God?
  Can even a wise man be of use to him?

³ 'Is it any pleasure to Shaddai, that you are righteous?
  Or is it profit to him that your ways are blameless?

⁴ 'Is it because of your fear of him that he corrects you
  and enters into judgment with you?

⁵ 'Is not your wickedness great,
  and are not your iniquities infinite?

⁶ 'Because you have demanded collateral from your
  brother without cause
  and stripped the naked of their clothing;

⁷ 'you have not given water to the weary to drink,
  and you have withheld bread from the hungry;

⁸ 'and the powerful possess the land,
  and the favored live in it;

⁹ 'widows you have sent away empty,
  and the strength of the fatherless is crushed;

10 'therefore, snares are all around you,
and sudden dread terrifies you;
11 'or darkness, so that you cannot see,
and a flood of waters covers you.
12 'Is not God in the height of heaven;
and look at the highest stars, are they not exalted?
13 'And you say, "What does God know;
can he judge from behind a dark cloud?
14 'Thick clouds are his covering, so he cannot see;
and he walks above the circle of heaven".
15 'Will you continue on the old path
where the wicked have trod?
16 'Those who were snatched away before their time,
a river swept away their foundation.
17 'Those who say to God, "Depart from us!"
and "What can Shaddai do about it?"
18 'Yet he filled their houses with good things,
but the counsel of the wicked is far from me.
19 'The righteous see it and are glad,
and the innocent ridicule
20 'saying, "Surely our adversaries[a] are destroyed,
and the fire consumes what remains of them".
21 'Get along well with him and be at peace;
thereby good will come to you.
22 'Receive instruction from his mouth,
and place his words in your heart.
23 'If you return to Shaddai, you will be built up;
when you put away injustice far from your tent,
24 'and when you value gold no more than dust,
and the gold of Ophir as stones in the river.
25 'Then Shaddai will be your gold
and your choice silver;

---

[a] The LXX reads, *substance* instead of *adversaries*.

²⁶ 'because then you will delight in Shaddai,
  and will lift up your face to God.
²⁷ 'You will pray to him, and he will hear you,
  and you will fulfill your vows.
²⁸ 'You will decide a thing, and it will be
  established for you,
  and light will shine on your paths.
²⁹ 'When people are brought low, you say it is arrogance;
  but he saves the humble person.
³⁰ 'He will even rescue one who is not innocent;
  he will be rescued by the purity of your hands'.

Chapter 23

Job Replies to Eliphaz's Third Speech
¹ Then Job answered and said,
² 'Today also my complaint is defiant.
  I force myself^a to keep on groaning.
³ 'O that I knew where I might find him,
  that I might come to his home.
⁴ 'I would present my case before him,
  and fill my mouth with arguments.
⁵ 'I would know the words which he would answer me,
  and I would understand what he would say to me.
⁶ 'Would he contend with me through the use of force?
  No, surely he would pay attention to me.
⁷ 'There the upright could reason with him;
  and I would be delivered by my judge.
⁸ 'Look, I go forward, but he is not there;
  and backward, but I cannot perceive him.

---

^a The Hebrew states, *my hand is heavy*, which I take to mean the use of force. That is, it takes all his power to continue groaning, because he is exhausted.

⁹ 'When he works on the left hand, I do not behold him;
   he turns to the right hand, and I do not see him,
¹⁰ 'but he knows the way that I take;
   when he has tested me, I will come out like gold.
¹¹ 'My foot has held fast to his path;
   I have kept his way and have not turned aside.
¹² 'I have not departed from the commandment
   of his lips;
   I have stored up^a the words of his mouth more
   than my necessary food.
¹³ 'But he is single-minded,^b and who can turn him?
   And what he desires, that he does;
¹⁴ 'because he completes what is appointed for me,
   and many such things are with him.
¹⁵ 'Therefore, am I terrified by his presence;
   I consider, and I tremble because of him;
¹⁶ 'and God has made my heart faint,
   and Shaddai has terrified me;
¹⁷ 'but I have not been silenced by the face of darkness,
   nor by the deep gloom that covers my face.

Chapter 24

Job Complains that God Is Inattentive

¹ 'Why are times not stored up by Shaddai,
   and why do they that know him not see his days?
² 'Some remove the landmarks;
   they violently take away flocks and pasture them.
³ 'They drive away the donkey of the orphan;
   they demand the widow's ox as security for a loan.

---

^a Lit. *I have hidden.*
^b The Hebrew states literally, *he is one.*

4 'They push the needy off the road;
  the poor of the land are forced to hide.
5 'Look, like wild donkeys in the wilderness,
  they go out to their work, rising early seeking game;
  the wilderness yields food for them and
  for their children.
6 'They gather fodder in the field,
  and they glean in the vineyard of the wicked.
7 'They spend the night naked, without clothing,
  and they have no covering in the cold.
8 'They are wet with the showers of the mountains,
  and without refuge, they cling to a rock.
9 'Others snatch the fatherless child from the breast,
  and demand from the poor security for a loan.
10 'So the poor go about naked, without clothing;
  hungry, they carry grain for others.
11 'Between the walls, they press out oil;
  they tread the winepresses, but they suffer thirst.
12 'From the city people groan,
  and the soul of the wounded cries out for help;
  and God does not regard their pleas to be improper.
13 'Others are among those who rebel against the light;
  they do not recognize its ways,
  and they do stay in its paths.
14 'At first light, the murderer rises;
  he kills the poor and needy;
  and in the night he is like a thief.
15 'Also the eye of the adulterer waits for the twilight,
  saying, "No eye will see me";
  and he puts a mask over his face.
16 'In the dark they break into houses;
  by day they shut themselves in;
  they do not know the light;

¹⁷ 'because the morning is the same to
  them as deep darkness;
  because they are friends with the terrors of
  deep darkness.
¹⁸ 'They are scum^a on the surface of the waters;
  their portion in the land is cursed;
  they do not turn toward the way of the vineyards.
¹⁹ 'Drought and heat snatch away the snow waters;
  so does Sheol those who have sinned.
²⁰ 'The womb forgets them; the worm finds them sweet;
  they will be remembered no more;
  and injustice will be broken like a tree.
²¹ 'They prey on^b the barren who do not bear,
  and they do no good to the widow.
²² 'God drags away the mighty by his power;
  they rise up, but no one is sure of life.
²³ 'He gives them security, and they rely on it;
  and his eyes are on their ways.
²⁴ 'They are exalted for a little while and then are gone;
  they are brought low and are gathered up like all others,
  and are cut off as the tops of the grain.
²⁵ 'If it is not so, who will prove me a liar
  and make my speech worthless?'

Chapter 25

Bildad's Third Speech: Only God Is Righteous
¹ Then Bildad the Shuhite answered and said,
² 'Dominion and awe belong to God;
  he makes peace in the heights of heaven.

---

^a The Hebrew can refer to something light and insignificant, which could be the scum that floats on top of the water.
^b The Hebrew says, *feed on.*

3 'Is there any number to his troops,
  and upon whom does his light not arise?
4 'How can a man be justified with God,
  and how can he that is born of a woman be clean?
5 'Indeed, even the moon is not bright,
  and the stars are not pure in his sight;
6 'how much less a man, who is a maggot,
  and the son of man, who is a worm'.

Chapter 26

Job Replies to Bildad's Third Speech
1 Then Job answered and said,
2 'How you have helped him who is without power;
  you have saved the arm that has no strength!
3 'How you have counseled him who has no wisdom;
  and you have declared sound advice in abundance!
4 'With whose help have you uttered words,
  and whose breath has come out from you?
5 'The departed spirits tremble
  under the waters and their inhabitants.
6 'Sheol is naked before God,
  and Abaddon[a] has no covering.
7 'He stretches out the north over empty space;
  he hangs the earth upon nothing.
8 'He binds up the waters in his thick clouds;
  and the cloud is not split open under them.
9 'He covers the face of his throne,
  and spreads his cloud over it.

---

[a] Abaddon, which means *destruction*, is another name for the place of
death. See Rev. 9.11.

¹⁰ 'He draws a circular boundary on the
    surface of the waters,
    at the boundary of light and darkness.
¹¹ 'The pillars of heaven[a] tremble
    and are astounded at his rebuke.
¹² 'By his power he stirred up the sea,[b]
    and with his skill he crushed Rahab.[c]
¹³ 'By his spirit the sky became clear;
    his hand pierced the fleeing serpent.
¹⁴ 'Indeed, these are but the fringes of his ways,
    and how small a whisper we hear of him;
    and his mighty thunder, who can understand?'

Chapter 27

Job Maintains His Integrity

¹ Then Job continued his discourse and said,
² 'As God lives, who has taken away my judgment;
    and Shaddai, who has made my entire being bitter;
³ 'as long as my breath is in me,
    and the spirit of God is in my nostrils,
⁴ 'my lips will not speak injustice,
    and my tongue will not utter deceit.
⁵ 'Far be it from me to say that you are right;
    until I die I will not put away my integrity from me.
⁶ 'I hold fast my righteousness and I will not let it go;
    my heart will not reproach me as long as I live.

---

[a] In poetic imagination, the sky is supported by pillars at earth's edge.

[b] Compare Isa. 51.15 and Jer. 31.35.

[c] The word *Rahab* means *arrogance.* It is used here and in other Scriptures as a symbol of evil personified (see Ps. 89.11, Isa. 51.9). It can also refer to Egypt (Isa. 30.7; Ps. 87.4).

7 'May my enemy be like the wicked,
and may he who rises up against me
be like the unrighteous.

8 'For what is the hope of the godless when he is cut off,
when God takes away his life?

9 'Will God hear his cry
when trouble comes upon him?

10 'Will he delight himself in Shaddai?
Will he call upon God at all times?

11 'I will teach you about the hand of God;
what is with Shaddai I will not conceal.

12 'Look, all of you have seen it yourselves;
why then have you become altogether vain?

13 'This is the wicked man's portion from God
and the oppressors' inheritance from Shaddai.

14 'If his children are multiplied, it is for the sword,
and his offspring will not have enough bread.

15 'His survivors will be buried in the plague,
and their widows will not weep.

16 'Though he heaps up silver like the dust,
and piles up clothing like the clay;

17 'he may pile it up, but the righteous will wear it;
and the innocent will divide the silver.

18 'He builds his house like a moth[a]
and like a booth that a watchman makes.

19 'Wealthy, he lies down, but will do so no more;
he opens his eyes, and all is gone.

20 'Terrors overtake him like flood waters;
a wind storm steals him away in the night.

21 'The east wind carries him away, and he departs;
it sweeps him out of his place.

---

[a] The LXX reads, *spider.*

²² 'It thrusts upon him without pity;
from its power, he surely flees.
²³ 'It claps its hands at him,
and it hisses at him from its place'.

PART VI:
JOB PRAISES THE MYSTERIES OF WISDOM (28.1-28)

Chapter 28

Job Ponders the Source Wisdom

1 'Surely there is a mine for the silver,
   and a place where they refine gold.
2 'Iron is taken out of the earth,[a]
   and copper is smelted from ore.
3 'Man puts an end to darkness
   and searches every extremity
   for ore in the darkness and the deep darkness.
4 'He breaks open a shaft away from where people live,
   in places forgotten by travelers;
   they hang and swing to and fro far from men.
5 'As for the earth, from it comes bread,
   and underneath, it is turned up as by fire.
6 'Its stones are the source of sapphires,
   and its dust contains gold.
7 'The path no bird of prey knows,
   and the falcon's eye has not seen it.

---

[a] Literally, *dust.*

⁸ 'The proud beasts^a have not trodden it,
    nor has the lion passed over it.
⁹ 'He puts forth his hand on the flinty rock;
    he overturns the mountains by the roots.
¹⁰ 'He cuts out channels in the rocks,
    and his eye sees every precious thing.
¹¹ 'He binds the floods from flowing,
    and what is hidden he brings to light.
¹² 'But where will wisdom be found?
    And where is the place of understanding?
¹³ 'Humans do not know its value,
    and it is not found in the land of the living.
¹⁴ 'The deep^b says, "It is not in me",
    and the sea says, "It is not with me".
¹⁵ 'It cannot be gotten for gold,
    nor can silver be weighed for its price.
¹⁶ 'It cannot be valued in the gold of Ophir,
    with the precious onyx or sapphire.
¹⁷ 'The gold and the glass cannot equal it,
    and it cannot be exchanged for jewels of fine gold.
¹⁸ 'No mention will be made of coral or crystal,
    and the price of wisdom is more than pearls.
¹⁹ 'The topaz of Ethiopia^c will not equal it;
    it cannot be valued in pure gold.
²⁰ 'From where then does wisdom come,
    and where is the place of understanding?
²¹ 'It is hidden from the eyes of all living
    and concealed from the birds of the air.

---

^a The Hebrew reads, *sons of pride.*

^b *The deep* refers here to very bottom of the sea (see Jon. 2.3, 'For you hurled me into the deep, into the heart of the sea, and the floods surrounded me; all your billows and your waves swept over me').

^c The Hebrew is *Cush*, which at one time was called Nubia, and is the area known now as Ethiopia.

22 'Abaddon[a] and death say,
  "We have heard reports of it with our ears".
23 'God understands the way to it;
  and he, indeed, knows its place;
24 'because he looks to the ends of the earth
  and sees everything under heaven.
25 'When he established the force[b] of the wind,
  and he measured out the waters;
26 'when he made a decree for the rain,
  and a path for the thunderbolt;
27 'then he saw it and declared it;
  he established it and also searched it out.
28 'And he said to humankind,
  "Look, the fear of Yahweh, that is wisdom;
  and to depart from evil is understanding".'

---

[a] Abaddon, which means *destruction*, is another name for the place of death. See Rev. 9.11.

[b] The Hebrew is lit., *weight*.

PART VII:
JOB IS STEADFAST IN HIS DEFENSE (29.1-31.40)

Chapter 29

Job Finishes His Defense

¹ Then Job continued his discourse and said,

² 'Oh, that it was like previous months,
  like the days when God watched over me,

³ 'when his lamp shone over my head,
  when by his light I walked through darkness;

⁴ 'like I was in the days of my youth,
  when the friendly counsel of God was over my tent;

⁵ 'when Shaddai was still with me,
  when my children were around me;

⁶ 'when my steps were bathed in cream,
  and the rock poured out rivers of oil for me;

⁷ 'when I went out to the gate of the city,
  when I took my seat in the square!

⁸ 'The young men saw me and hid themselves:
  and the aged rose and stood up.

⁹ 'The princes refrained talking,
  and put their hand on their mouth.

¹⁰ 'The nobles held their peace,
  and their tongue stuck to the roof of their mouth.

¹¹ 'When the ear heard, then it blessed me;
   and when the eye saw, then it approved me;
¹² 'when I delivered the poor that cried for help
   and the fatherless and him that had none to help him.
¹³ 'The blessing of the perishing man came upon me,
   and I caused the widow's heart to sing for joy.
¹⁴ 'I put on righteousness, and it clothed me;
   my judgment was like a robe and a diadem.
¹⁵ 'I was eyes for the blind,
   and I was feet for the lame.
¹⁶ 'I was a father to the poor,
   and I investigated the case that I did not know.
¹⁷ 'I broke the jaws of the wicked
   and snatched the victim from his teeth.
¹⁸ 'Then I said, "I shall die in my nest,
   and I shall multiply my days as the sand.
¹⁹ "My root was spread out by the waters,
   and the dew lay all night upon my branch.
²⁰ "My glory was fresh in me,
   and my bow was renewed in my hand".
²¹ 'They listened to me and waited
   and kept silence for my counsel.
²² 'After my words they did not speak again,
   and my speech settled on them like dew.
²³ 'They waited for me as for the rain,
   and they opened their mouths as for the latter rain.
²⁴ 'I smiled on them when they did not believe,
   and the light of my countenance
   they did not cast down.
²⁵ 'I chose their way and sat as chief;
   and I lived as a king among the troops,
   like one who comforts mourners.

Chapter 30

Job Feels Humiliated

¹ 'But now those who are younger than I mock me,
  whose fathers I disdained to put
  with the dogs of my flock.

² 'Also, how does the strength of their hands profit me;
  they whose vigor has perished?

³ 'In need and in hard famine, they gnaw the dry ground
  by night in ruin and devastation;

⁴ 'they pluck leaves from a bush
  and roots of the broom-shrub for their food.

⁵ 'They are driven out from community;
  they shout at them as at a thief,

⁶ 'to dwell in the slopes of the river beds,
  in caves of the earth and in the rocks.

⁷ 'Among the bushes they bray;
  under the nettles they gather together.

⁸ 'Children of fools and of the nameless,
  they were whipped out of the land.

⁹ 'Now am I their taunting song;
  yes, I have become their byword.

¹⁰ 'They abhor me; they keep their distance from me,
  and they do not hesitate to spit in my face.

¹¹ 'Because God has loosed my bowstring,
  and afflicted me,
  they have cast off the bridle before me.

¹² 'At my right hand their brood arises;
  they push away my feet,
  and they raise against me their ways of destruction.

¹³ 'They tear apart my path;
  they promote my calamity;
  they need no one help them.

¹⁴ 'As through a wide breach they come;
   like a storm they roll over me.
¹⁵ 'Terrors are turned on me;
   they pursue my dignity like the wind,
   and my salvation passes away as a cloud.
¹⁶ 'Now my whole being is poured out within me;
   the days of affliction have taken hold of me.
¹⁷ 'At night, my bones are pierced in me,
   and gnawing pain never stops.
¹⁸ 'By the great force my garment is distorted;
   it binds me about as the collar of my coat.
¹⁹ 'He has cast me into the mire,
   and I have become like dust and ashes.
²⁰ 'I cry to you for help, but you do not answer me;
   I stand up, and you just look at me.
²¹ 'You have become cruel to me;
   with your strong hand you oppose me.
²² 'You lift me up on the wind; you cause me to ride on it;
   and you tear me apart in the storm.
²³ 'For I know that you will bring me to death
   and to the house appointed for all living.
²⁴ 'Surely, does not one in ruins stretch out his hand,
   when in his disaster, therefore, he cries out for help?
²⁵ 'Did I not weep for him who was in trouble?
   Was not my whole being grieved for the poor?
²⁶ 'When I hoped for good, then disaster came upon me;
   and when I waited for light, darkness came.
²⁷ 'My insides boil and do not rest;
   days of affliction come to meet me.
²⁸ 'In darkness I walk around, without the sun;
   I stand up in the assembly, and I cry for help.
²⁹ 'I am a brother to jackals,
   and a companion of ostriches.

30 'My skin turns black and peels off,
   and my bones burn with fever.
31 'My lyre plays only sad music,
   and my flute sounds like weeping.

Chapter 31

Job Testifies of His Faithfulness

1 'I made a covenant with my eyes;
   how, then, could I gaze at a virgin?
2 'And what is my portion from God above?
   and my inheritance from Shaddai on high?
3 'Does not disaster belong to the wicked,
   and calamity to the workers of iniquity?
4 'Does he not see my ways,
   and count all my steps?
5 'If I have walked in vanity,
   or if my foot has hurried after deceit,
6 'let me be weighed in an accurate balance,
   and let God know my integrity.
7 'If my step has turned away from the path,
   and my heart has pursued the sights of my eyes,
   and if any stain clings to my hands,
8 'then let me sow, but let another eat;
   yes, let my offspring be rooted out.
9 'If my heart has gone after a woman,
   or if I have laid wait at my neighbor's door,
10 'then let my wife grind for another,
   and let others kneel down over her.
11 'Because that is shameful behavior;
   and it is iniquity that should be punished.

¹² 'Because it is a fire that would consume to Abaddon,ᵃ
and it would eradicate all my harvest.

¹³ 'If I have refused justice for my male or female servant
when they pleaded with me,

¹⁴ 'what, then, shall I do when God rises up;
and when he examines, what shall I answer him?

¹⁵ 'Did not he who made me in the womb make him;
and did not the same one fashion us in the womb?

¹⁶ 'If I have hindered the poor from their desire,
or have caused the eyes of the widow to fail;

¹⁷ 'or have eaten my morsel alone,
and the orphan has not eaten of it—

¹⁸ 'but from my youth he was brought up
with me as with a father,
and I guided the widow from my mother's womb—

¹⁹ 'if I have seen anyone perish for lack of clothing,
or any poor person without covering,

²⁰ 'if his loins have not blessed me,
and he was not warmed with the fleece of my sheep,

²¹ 'if I have raised my hand against the orphan,
when I saw I had support in the gate,

²² 'let my shoulder fall from its socket,
and let my arm be broken from the elbow.

²³ 'because disaster from God is a terror to me,
and I am powerless before his majesty.

²⁴ 'If I have made gold my confidence,
or thought of fine gold as my security,

²⁵ 'if I rejoiced because my wealth was great,
and because my hand had gained much,

²⁶ 'if I saw the sun when it shone,
or the moon moving in splendor;

ᵃ Abaddon, which means *destruction*, is another name for the place of
death. See Rev. 9.11.

²⁷ 'and my heart has been secretly enticed,
   and my mouth has kissed my hand,
²⁸ 'that also would be iniquity that should be punished,
   because I would have denied God above.
²⁹ 'If I rejoiced at the destruction of him who hated me,
   or exalted myself when disaster found him—
³⁰ 'I have not allowed my mouth to sin
   by wishing for a curse on his life—
³¹ 'if those in my tent ever said,
   "Oh, that we might be satisfied with his meat".
³² '—the stranger has not lodged in the street,
   I have opened my doors to the traveler^a—
³³ 'if I covered my transgressions like Adam,
   by hiding my iniquity in my bosom,
³⁴ 'because I feared the great multitude,
   and the contempt of families terrified me,
   so that I kept silence, and did not go out of doors—
³⁵ 'Oh, that one would hear me!
   Here is my signature! Let Shaddai answer me!
   And here is the indictment written by my accuser!
³⁶ 'Surely, I would carry it on my shoulder
   and bind it on me like a crown.
³⁷ 'I would declare to him the number of my steps;
   like a prince I would approach him.
³⁸ 'If my land has cried out against me,
   and its furrows have wept together,
³⁹ 'if I have eaten its fruit without payment,
   or caused its owners to breathe their last;
⁴⁰ 'Let briars grow instead of wheat,
   and weeds instead of barley'.
The words of Job are ended.

---

^a *Traveler* is the reading of the LXX; the MT says, *road.*

PART VIII:
ELIHU ACCUSES JOB FURTHER (32.1-37.24)

Chapter 32

Elihu Rebukes Eliphaz, Bildad, and Zophar

¹ So these three men ceased answering Job, because he was righteous in his own eyes.

² Then great anger was aroused in Elihu the son of Barachel the Buzite, of the family of Ram.ᵃ His anger burned against Job because he justified himself rather than God.

³ His anger was aroused also against his three friends because they had found no answer and yet had condemned Job.

⁴ Now Elihu had waited to speak to Job because they were years older than he.

⁵ When Elihu saw that there was no answer in the mouth of these three men, then his anger was aroused.

⁶ And Elihu the son of Barachel the Buzite answered and said:

'I am young in years, and you are aged;
    therefore I was afraid
    and dared not show you my opinion.

ᵃ Although Elihu is introduced here for the first time, his comments reveal that he had been present for much, if not all, of the previous debate between Job, Eliphaz, Bildad, and Zophar.

⁷ 'I thought, "Age should speak,
and many years teach wisdom".
⁸ 'Surely, it is the spirit in mankind,
and the breath of Shaddai that gives them
understanding.
⁹ 'It is not the old that are wise,
nor do elders understand what is right.
¹⁰ 'Therefore I say,
"Listen to me; I also will tell what I know".
¹¹ 'Look, I waited for your words;
I listened to your reasonings,
while you searched out what to say.
¹² 'I paid attention to you,
and, surely, none of you convinced Job
nor answered his words.
¹³ 'Do not say, "We have found wisdom;
God, not man, will subdue him".
¹⁴ 'He has not directed his words against me,
so I will not answer him with your speeches.
¹⁵ 'They are dismayed; they answer no more;
words escape them.
¹⁶ 'Shall I wait, because they do not speak,
because they stand still and answer no more?
¹⁷ 'I also will answer my part;
I too will tell what I know.
¹⁸ 'For I am full of words,
the spirit within me compels me.
¹⁹ 'Look, my belly is like wine that has no vent;
it is ready to burst like new wineskins.
²⁰ 'I must speak, that I may get relief;
I must open my lips and answer.
²¹ 'May I never show partiality,
nor use flattery toward anyone.

22 'For I do not know how to flatter;
   or my maker would soon take me away.

Chapter 33

Elihu Claims to Speak for God
1 'But now, Job, please hear my speech,
   and listen to all my words.
2 'Please look, I open my mouth;
   my tongue speaks in my mouth.
3 'My words are from the uprightness of my heart,
   and my lips utter knowledge clearly.
4 'The spirit of God made me,
   and the breath of Shaddai gives me life.
5 'Answer me, if you can;
   set your words in order before me, take your stand.
6 'Surely, I am like you before God;
   I also am formed out of the clay.
7 'Indeed, no dread of me should terrify you,
   nor should my pressure be heavy upon you.
8 'Surely you have spoken in my hearing,
   and I have heard the sound of your words:
9 "I am clean, without transgression;
   I am innocent, nor is there iniquity in me.
10 "Look, he finds occasions against me;
   he counts me as his enemy;
11 "he puts my feet in the stocks;
   he watches all my paths".
12 'Look, in this you are not right; I will answer you,
   because God is greater than any human.
13 'Why do you complain against him
   that he does not account for all his doings?
14 'Indeed, God speaks once, even twice,
   yet no one perceives it.

¹⁵ 'In a dream, in a vision of the night,
   when deep sleep falls upon people,
   while slumbering on their beds,
¹⁶ 'then he opens the ears of people,
   and seals their instruction,
¹⁷ 'to turn aside people from their purpose,
   and conceal pride from them;
¹⁸ 'to spare their souls from the Pit,^a
   and their lives from perishing by the sword.^b
¹⁹ 'He is chastened with pain upon his bed
   and continual suffering in his bones,
²⁰ 'so that his life loathes bread,
   and his appetite the finest food.
²¹ 'His flesh wastes away from sight,
   and his bones that were not seen stick out.
²² 'His soul draws near to the Pit,
   and his life to those who bring death.
²³ 'If there is an angel for him,
   a mediator, one among a thousand,
   to declare a person upright,
²⁴ 'and he is gracious to him, and says,
   "Deliver him from going down to the Pit;
   I have found a ransom;
²⁵ "let his flesh become fresher than a child's;
   let him return to the days of his youth".
²⁶ 'Then he will pray to God,
   and he will be favorable to him,
   and he will see his face with joy,
   and he will repay him for his righteousness.

---

^a The 'Pit' refers to the entrance to Sheol.

^b See also Job 36.12.

27 'He will look upon others and say,
   "I have sinned and perverted what was right,
   and it did not profit me.
28 "He redeemed my soul from going down to the Pit,
   and my life will see the light".
29 'Behold, God works all these things,
   twice, three times with a person,
30 'to bring back his soul from the Pit,
   to be enlightened with the light of the living.
31 'Pay attention, Job, listen to me;
   hold your peace, and I will speak.
32 'If you have anything to say, answer me;
   speak, for I desire to justify you.
33 'If not, listen to me;
   keep silent, and I will teach you wisdom'.

Chapter 34

Elihu Affirms God's Justice

1 Elihu answered further and said,
2 'Hear my words, you wise men;
   and give ear to me, you who know;
3 'because the ear tests words,
   as the palate tastes food.
4 'Let us choose for ourselves what is right;
   let us know among ourselves what is good.
5 'For Job has said, "I am righteous,
   but God has taken away my judgment;
6 "though I am just, I am counted a liar;
   my wound[a] is incurable,
   though I am without transgression".

---

[a] The Hebrew is *arrow*, which I take to be a figure of speech that means the wound caused by an arrow.

⁷ 'What man is like Job,
    who drinks scorn like water,
⁸ 'who goes in company with the workers of iniquity
    and walks with wicked men?
⁹ 'Because he has said, "It profits a man nothing
    that he should delight himself in God".
¹⁰ 'Therefore listen to me, you men of understanding,
    far be it from God that he would do wickedness,
    and from Shaddai that he would do wrong.
¹¹ 'He will repay a man for his work
    and will cause him to find what befits his behavior.
¹² 'Surely, God will not do wickedly,
    and Shaddai will not pervert judgment.
¹³ 'Who gave him charge over the earth,
    and who laid on him the whole world?
¹⁴ 'If he should set his heart to it,
    and gather to himself his spirit and his breath,
¹⁵ 'all flesh would perish together,
    and man would return to dust.
¹⁶ 'If you have understanding, hear this;
    listen to the sound of my words.
¹⁷ 'Should one who hates justice govern,
    and will you condemn him that is most just?
¹⁸ 'Who says to a king, "You are worthless",
    and to rulers, "You are wicked?"
¹⁹ 'Who shows no partiality to princes,
    nor regards the rich more than the poor,
    for they all are the work of his hands?
²⁰ 'In a moment they die,
    and at midnight they are shaken and pass away,
    and the mighty are taken away without a hand.
²¹ 'For God's eyes are upon the ways of a man,
    and he sees all his steps.

²² 'There is no darkness or deep shadow
 where the workers of evil may hide themselves.
²³ 'For he has not appointed a time for anyone,
 to go before God in judgment.
²⁴ 'He breaks in pieces mighty ones without investigation
 and sets others in their place.
²⁵ 'Therefore he knows their works,
 and he overturns them in the night,
 and they are crushed.
²⁶ 'He strikes them like the wicked
 in the open sight of others,
²⁷ 'because they turned aside from following him
 and did not regard any of his ways,
²⁸ 'so that they cause the cry of the poor to come to him,
 and he heard the cry of the afflicted—
²⁹ 'When he keeps quiet, who then can condemn?
 And when he hides his face, who can behold him,
 whether it be a nation or an individual?—
³⁰ 'so that the godless should not rule,
 or ensnare the people.
³¹ 'Has anyone said to God,
 "I have borne punishment;
 I will offend no more;
³² "teach me what I do not see;
 if I have done iniquity, I will do it no more"?
³³ 'Will he then repay on your terms, because
 you refused it?
 For you must choose, and not I;
 therefore, speak what you know.
³⁴ 'People of understanding will say to me,
 and the wise who hear me,
³⁵ "Job speaks without knowledge,
 and his words are without insight".

³⁶ 'Would that Job were tried to the limit,
  because his answers are like those of the wicked,
³⁷ 'because he adds rebellion to his sin;
  he claps his hands among us,
  and multiplies his words against God'.

Chapter 35

Elihu Condemns Job
¹ Moreover, Elihu answered and said,
² 'Do you think this is just?
  You say, "I am right before God".
³ 'When you say, "What advantage will it be to you?
  What profit will I have more than if I had sinned?"
⁴ 'I will answer you,
  and your friends with you.
⁵ 'Look at the heavens and see,
  and observe the clouds—they are higher than you.
⁶ 'If you sin, what do you accomplish against him?
  Or if your transgressions are multiplied,
  what do you do to him?
⁷ 'If you are righteous, what do you give him?
  Or, what does he receive from your hand?
⁸ 'Your wickedness is for a man like you;
  and your righteousness for a son of man.
⁹ 'Because of the many oppressions they cry out;
  they cry for help because of the arm of the mighty.
¹⁰ 'But none says, "Where is God my maker,
  who gives songs in the night,
¹¹ "who teaches us more than the beasts of the earth,
  and makes us wiser than the birds of heaven?"
¹² 'There they cry out, but he does not answer,
  because of the pride of evil men.

¹³ 'Surely God does not hear an empty cry,
   and Shaddai does not regard it.
¹⁴ 'How much less when you say you do not see him,
   yet judgment is before him;
   and you must wait anxiously for him.
¹⁵ 'And now, because he has not punished in his anger,
   and he has not acknowledged folly,
¹⁶ 'Job opens his mouth in empty talk;
   he multiplies words without knowledge'.

Chapter 36

Elihu Extols God's Greatness

¹ Elihu continued and said,
² 'Bear with me a little, and I will show you
   that there is more to be said on God's behalf.
³ 'I will bring my knowledge from afar,
   and I will ascribe righteousness to my maker.
⁴ 'For truly my words are not false;
   one who has perfect knowledge is with you.
⁵ 'Behold, God is mighty and despises no one;
   he is mighty in strength of understanding.
⁶ 'He does not preserve the life of the wicked
   but gives justice to the needy.
⁷ 'He does not withdraw his eyes from the righteous,
   but with kings on the throne
   he sets them forever, and they are exalted.
⁸ 'If they are bound in fetters,
   and caught in cords of affliction,
⁹ 'Then he declares to them their work
   and their transgressions, because they are arrogant.
¹⁰ 'He opens their ear to discipline,
   and he says they should turn from evil.

¹¹ 'If they obey and they serve him,
     they will finish their days in prosperity
     and their years in contentment;
¹² 'but if they do not obey, they shall perish by the sword,
     and they shall die without knowledge.
¹³ 'The godless in heart heap up anger;
     they do not cry for help when he binds them.
¹⁴ 'They die in youth,
     and their life ends among the cult prostitutes.
¹⁵ 'He delivers the needy in their affliction,
     and he opens their ears in times of oppression.
¹⁶ 'Surely, he drew you out of distress
     into a broad place where there is no constraint;
     and what was set on your table was full of richness.
¹⁷ 'But you are full of judgment on the wicked;
     judgment and justice take hold of you.
¹⁸ 'Beware lest wrath draw you into scoffing,
     and do not let a great ransom turn you aside.
¹⁹ 'Will your wealth keep you from distress,
     or all the force of your strength?
²⁰ 'Do not long for the night,
     when people are cut off in their place.
²¹ 'Take care, do not turn to evil,
     because you have chosen this rather than affliction.
²² 'Behold, God is exalted in his power;
     who is a teacher like him?
²³ 'Who has prescribed his way for him,
     and who has said, "You have done wrong"?
²⁴ 'Remember to magnify his work
     of which people have sung.
²⁵ 'Everyone has seen it;
     everyone beholds it from afar.
²⁶ 'Surely, God is great, and we do not know him,
     the number of his years is unsearchable.

²⁷ 'When he draws up the drops of water,
   they distil rain from the mist,

²⁸ 'which the clouds pour down
   and drop on people abundantly.

²⁹ 'Can anyone understand the spreading of clouds,
   the thunderings of his pavilion?

³⁰ 'See, he spreads his lightning around him,
   and he covers the depths of the sea.

³¹ 'For by these he judges the people;
   he gives food in abundance.

³² 'He covers his hands with the lightning,
   and commands it to strike the mark.

³³ 'His thunder declares it;
   the cattle also know it is coming.

Chapter 37

Elihu Proclaims God's Majesty

¹ 'At this also my heart trembles
   and leaps out of its place.

² 'Listen attentively to the thunder of his voice
   and the rumbling that goes out of his mouth.

³ 'Under the whole heaven he lets it loose,
   and his lightning to the ends of the earth.

⁴ 'After it a voice roars;
   he thunders with his majestic voice,
   and he does not restrain them when his voice is heard.

⁵ 'God thunders marvelously with his voice;
   he does great things which we cannot comprehend.

⁶ 'For he says to the snow, "Fall on the earth".
   Likewise to the rain and to his mighty downpour.

⁷ 'He seals up the hand^a of every person,
    that everyone may know his work.
⁸ 'Then the beasts go into dens
    and remain in their lairs.
⁹ 'Out of the south comes the whirlwind
    and cold out of the north;
¹⁰ 'By the breath of God ice is given,
    and the broad waters are frozen.
¹¹ 'Also, he loads the thick cloud with moisture;
    the clouds scatter his lightning.
¹² 'They are turned about by his guidance,
    that they may do whatever he commands them
    on the face of the inhabited earth.
¹³ 'Whether for correction or for his land,
    or for steadfast love, he causes it to happen.
¹⁴ 'Listen to this, Job,
    stand and consider the wondrous works of God.
¹⁵ 'Do you know when God dispatches them
    and causes the lightning of his cloud to shine?
¹⁶ 'Do you know how the clouds are balanced,
    the wondrous works of him who is
    perfect in knowledge,
¹⁷ 'you, who swelter in your clothes
    when the earth is still because of the south wind?
¹⁸ 'Can you, like him, spread out the skies,
    strong like a molten mirror?^b
¹⁹ 'Teach us what we shall say to him;
    we cannot prepare our speech because of darkness.

---

^a The probable meaning of this verse is that when God sends rain and snow, he prevents people from working; thereby revealing his own divine work in nature.

^b In ancient times, mirrors were made of molten copper or bronze that was polished to a smooth reflective surface.

²⁰ 'Should it be told him that I want to speak?
   Did anyone ever wish to be swallowed up?
²¹ 'Now, no one can look on the bright light in the skies,
   when the wind has passed and cleared away the clouds.
²² 'Out of the north comes golden splendor;
   with God is awesome majesty.
²³ 'Shaddai—we cannot find him;
   he is great in power,
   and in judgment and in abundant righteousness;
   he will not afflict.
²⁴ 'Therefore, people fear him;
   he sees those who are wise in their own minds'.

PART IX:
GOD APPEARS IN A WHIRLWIND AND SPEAKS WITH AUTHORITY (38.1-41.34)

Chapter 38

Yahweh Speaks to Job

1 Then Yahweh answered Job out of the whirlwind
 and said,
2 'Who is this who darkens counsel[a]
 by words without knowledge?
3 'Prepare yourself[b] like a man;
 I will ask you, and you will make it known to me.
4 'Where were you when I founded the earth?
 Tell, if you have understanding.
5 'Who set its measurements, since you know?
 Or who stretched the line upon it?
6 'On what were its bases sunk,
 or who laid its cornerstone,
7 'when the morning stars sang together,
 and all the sons of God shouted for joy?

---

[a] *Counsel* refers to God's counsel, his plans. Therefore, this rhetorical question, directed to Job, accuses him of attempting to obscure God's plans, thus avoiding the truth.

[b] Hebrew, lit., *gird up your loins.*

⁸ 'Or who confined the sea with doors,
　　when it broke forth and went out of the womb,
⁹ 'when I made a cloud its garment,
　　and thick darkness its swaddling band,
¹⁰ 'and I placed boundaries on it,
　　and set bars and doors,
¹¹ 'and said, "This far you will come but no farther,
　　and here your proud waves will stop"?
¹² 'Have you commanded the morning in your days
　　and caused the dawn to know his place,
¹³ 'that it might take hold of the ends of the earth,
　　And that the wicked might be shaken out of it?
¹⁴ 'It is changed like clay under the seal,
　　and it stands out as a garment.
¹⁵ 'From the wicked their light is withheld,
　　and the uplifted arm is broken.
¹⁶ 'Have you entered into the springs of the sea,
　　or walked in the recesses of the depths?
¹⁷ 'Have the gates of death been revealed to you,
　　or have you seen the gates of deep darkness?
¹⁸ 'Have you understood the expanse of the earth?
　　Tell, if you know all this.
¹⁹ 'Where is the way to the dwelling of light,
　　and as for darkness, where is its place,
²⁰ 'that you may take it to its territory,
　　and that you may discern the paths to its house?
²¹ 'You know, because you were born then,
　　And the number of your days is great!
²² 'Have you entered into the storehouses of the snow,
　　or have you seen the storehouses of the hail,
²³ 'which I have reserved for the time of trouble,
　　for the day of battle and war?
²⁴ 'By what way is the light diffused,
　　or the east wind scattered on the earth?

25 'Who has cut a channel for the flood,
　　or a path for the thunderbolt,
26 'to bring rain on a land where no one is,
　　even on the desert where no one lives,
27 'to satisfy the desolate wasteland,
　　and to make the ground sprout with grass?
28 'Does the rain have a father,
　　and who has begotten the drops of dew?
29 'From whose womb came the ice,
　　and the frost of heaven, who gave it birth?
30 'The waters harden like stone,
　　and the surface of the deep[a] is frozen.
31 'Can you tie the chains of the Pleiades,[b]
　　or loose the cords of Orion?
32 'Can you bring out the constellations in their season,
　　or guide the Bear with its children?
33 'Do you know the ordinances of the heavens?
　　Can you set their dominion over the earth?
34 'Can you lift up your voice to the clouds
　　so that an abundance of waters may cover you?
35 'Can you send lightnings that they may go
　　and say to you, "Here we are"?
36 'Who has put wisdom in the inward parts,
　　or who has given understanding to the mind?
37 'Who can number the clouds by wisdom,
　　or who can pour out the jars of heaven,
38 'when the dust turns into hard clumps,
　　and the clods stick together?
39 'Can you hunt the prey for the lion,
　　or fill the appetite of the young lions,

---

[a] The *deep* refers to the ocean, the depths of the sea (see Gen. 1.2).
[b] Pleiades, Orion, and the Bear are constellations of the stars.

40 'when they crouch in their dens
    or lie in the thicket to wait in ambush?
41 'Who provides for the raven his food,
    when his young ones cry to God for help,
    and they wander about for lack of food?

Chapter 39

God Declares His Power over Nature

1 'Do you know the time when the mountain goats give
    birth?
    Do you observe the calving of the deer?
2 'Can you number the months that they fulfill,
    and do you know the time when they give birth,
3 'when they crouch to give birth to their offspring,
    and are delivered of their young?ª
4 'Their offspring become strong;
    they grow up in the open;
    they go forth and do not return to them.
5 'Who sent out the wild donkey free?
    Who loosed the bonds of the swift donkey,
6 'to whom I gave the wilderness for a home,
    and the salt land for his dwelling?
7 'He scorns the tumult of the city;
    he does not hear the shouts of the driver.
8 'He seeks out the mountains as his pasture,
    and he searches after every green thing.
9 'Is the wild ox willing to serve you?
    Will he spend the night at your manger?
10 'Can you bind the wild ox in a furrow with ropes,
    and will he plow the valleys behind you?

ª The Hebrew reads lit., *pangs*, which I take to mean the pains of
childbirth.

¹¹ 'Will you trust him because his strength is great,
    and will you leave your labor to him?
¹² 'Will you have faith in him to bring home your grain
    and gather it to your threshing floor?
¹³ 'The ostrich's wings flap joyously,
    but not like the pinions and plumage of the stork,[a]
¹⁴ 'because she abandons her eggs to the earth,
    and lets them be warmed on the ground,
¹⁵ 'forgetting that a foot may crush them,
    and that the wild beast may trample them.
¹⁶ 'She is hardened against her young,
    as though they were not hers;
    though her labor be in vain, she is unconcerned,
¹⁷ 'because God has made her forget wisdom,
    and has not given her a portion of understanding.
¹⁸ 'When she lifts up herself on high,
    she laughs at the horse and his rider.
¹⁹ 'Do you give the horse its strength?
    Do you clothe it neck with a mane?
²⁰ 'Do you make it leap like a locust?
    Its majestic snorting is terrifying.
²¹ 'It paws in the valley and rejoices in its strength;
    it goes out to meet the weapons.
²² 'It laughs at fear and is not dismayed;
    and it does not turn back from the sword.
²³ 'On it rattles the quiver,
    the flashing spear and the javelin.
²⁴ 'With fierceness and rage, it swallows the ground;
    and it does not stand still at the sound of the trumpet.
²⁵ 'At the sound of the trumpet, he says, "Aha!"
    He smells the battle from afar,
    the thunder of the captains, and the shouting.

---

[a] The meaning of the Hebrew is uncertain.

²⁶ 'Does the hawk soar by your understanding
   and spread its wings toward the south?
²⁷ 'Does the eagle mount up at your command
   and make its nest on high?
²⁸ 'It dwells and lodges on the rock,
   on the rocky crag and strong place.
²⁹ 'From there it searches for prey;
   its eyes see it from far away.
³⁰ 'Her young ones also suck up blood,
   and where the slain are, there she is'.

Chapter 40

Should Job Argue with God?

¹ Moreover, Yahweh answered Job and said,
² 'Shall a faultfinder contend with Shaddai?
   He who argues with God, let him answer it'.
³ Then Job answered Yahweh and said,
⁴ 'Behold, I am insignificant; what shall I answer you?
   I lay my hand on my mouth.
⁵ 'I have spoken once, but I will not answer;
   twice, but not again'.

Yahweh Further Declares His Power

⁶ Then Yahweh answered Job out of the whirlwind
   and said,
⁷ 'Prepare yourselfᵃ like a man;
   I will ask you, and you will make it known to me.
⁸ 'Would you really questionᵇ my judgment?
   Will you condemn me that you may be right?
⁹ 'Have you an arm like God,
   and can you thunder with a voice like his?

ᵃ Literally, *gird up your loins.*

ᵇ That is, *nullify.*

¹⁰ 'Adorn yourself now with majesty and excellence,
  and array yourself with glory and beauty.
¹¹ 'Pour out the overflowing of your anger,
  and look on all the proud, and abase them.
¹² 'Look on all the proud and humble them,
  and tread down the wicked where they stand.
¹³ 'Hide them in the dust together;
  bind their faces in the hidden place.
¹⁴ 'Then I will also confess to you
  that your own right hand can save you.
¹⁵ 'Look now at Behemoth[a]
  which I made just like I made you;
  he eats grass like an ox.
¹⁶ 'See now his strength is in his loins,
  and his power is in the muscles of his belly.
¹⁷ 'He moves his tail like a cedar;
  the sinews of his thighs are knit together.
¹⁸ 'His bones are tubes of bronze;
  his limbs are like rods of iron.
¹⁹ 'He is the first of the ways of God;
  let him who made him bring near his sword.
²⁰ 'Surely the mountains bring him food,
  where all the beasts of the field play.
²¹ 'He lies down under the lotus trees,
  in the shelter of the reed and in the marsh;
²² 'The lotus trees cover him with shade;
  the willows of the brook surround him.
²³ 'See, the river rages, but he is not alarmed;
  he is confident though the Jordan rushes to his mouth.

---

[a] The word *behemoth* is the Hebrew plural of the word *beast*. Most scholars interpret Behemoth to represent the hippopotamus. The lack of exact correspondence to physical characteristics is not unusual, given that this text is poetry.

²⁴ 'Can one take him by his eyes,^a
   or pierce his nose with a snare.

Chapter 41

God's Power Displayed in His Creatures

¹ 'Can you draw out Leviathan^b with a fishhook
   or restrain his tongue with a cord?
² 'Can you put a rope in his nose,
   or pierce his jaw with a hook?
³ 'Will he make many supplications to you?
   Will he speak soft words to you?
⁴ 'Will he make a covenant with you?
   Will you take him for a servant forever?
⁵ 'Will you play with him as with a bird,
   or will you put him on a leash for your girls?
⁶ 'Will the traders bargain over him?
   Will they divide him up among the merchants?
⁷ 'Can you fill his skin with harpoons
   or his head with fishing spears?
⁸ 'Lay your hand on him;
   remember the battle, you will not do it again.

---

[a] This translation clearly reflects the Hebrew wording, but the meaning of the phrase 'take him by his eyes' is unclear. It could refer to the unlikely success of trying to spear him in the eye. Also, it could be an idiomatic phrase that means, 'Can one take him while he is watching?' Commentators are undecided.

[b] Leviathan is usually understood to represent the crocodile. However, because Leviathan seems to breathe fire (v. 19), some scholars take it to be a mythological creature. I would interpret the myth-like characteristics as poetic hyperbole. Hyperbole, a literary device common to Old Testament poetry, is an obvious exaggeration for the sake of emphasis (e.g. 'I am so hungry I could eat a horse'). The book of Job contains many examples of hyperbole; e.g. 6.2-4; 7.6; 12.2; 12.7; 40.18; 41.24

⁹ 'Look, any hope of overcoming him is in vain;
   shall not one be overwhelmed at the sight of him?
¹⁰ 'No one is so fierce that he dares to stir him up;
   who then is able to stand before me?
¹¹ 'Who has first given to me that I should repay him?
   Everything under heaven is mine.
¹² 'I will not be silent concerning his limbs,
   or his mighty strength, or his splendid frame.
¹³ 'Who can remove his outer garment?
   Who can approach him with a bridle?
¹⁴ 'Who can open the doors of his face?
   Terror is all around his teeth.
¹⁵ 'His scales are his pride,
   shut up tightly as with a seal.
¹⁶ 'One is so near to another
   that no air can come between them.
¹⁷ 'They are joined to each other;
   they stick together that they cannot be separated.
¹⁸ 'His sneezes flash forth light,
   and his eyes are like the eyelids of the dawn.
¹⁹ 'Out of his mouth go burning torches,
   and sparks of fire leap out.
²⁰ 'Out of his nostrils goes smoke,
   as out of a boiling pot or burning rushes.
²¹ 'His breath kindles coals,
   and a flame goes out of his mouth.
²² 'Strength lodges in his neck,
   and dances before him.
²³ 'The folds of his flesh are joined together;
   they are firm on him; they cannot be moved.
²⁴ 'His heart is as firm as a stone;
   as firm as the lower millstone.[a]

---

[a] The upper millstone rotates, but the lower millstone does not move.

²⁵ 'When he raises up himself, the mighty are afraid;
      at his crashing they are beside themselves.
²⁶ 'The sword that reaches him cannot avail,
      nor the spear, the arrow, or the javelin.
²⁷ 'He counts iron as straw
      and bronze as rotten wood.
²⁸ 'The arrow cannot make him flee;
      sling stones are turned into stubble by him.
²⁹ 'A club is counted as stubble;
      he laughs at the shaking of a javelin.
³⁰ 'His underparts are like sharp potsherds;
      he spreads out like a threshing sledge on the mire.
³¹ 'He makes the deep^a boil like a pot;
      he makes the sea like a jar of ointment.^b
³² 'He leaves a shining wake behind him;
      one would think the deep had white hair.^c
³³ 'On earth there is nothing like him,
      a creature without fear.
³⁴ 'He sees every lofty thing;
      he is king over all the sons of pride'.

---

^a The *deep* refers to the ocean, the depths of the sea (see Gen. 1.2).
Leviathan's thrashing about makes the ocean churn like a boiling pot.
^b The sea is stirred up as when someone is mixing ointment.
^c The frothy waves give the appearance of white hair.

PART X:
JOB'S REPUTATION, FAMILY, AND PROSPERITY ARE RESTORED (42.1-17)

Chapter 42

Job's Confession and Repentance

¹ Then Job answered Yahweh and said,

² 'I know that you can do all things,
   and no purpose of yours can be thwarted.

³ 'You asked, "Who is this who hides counsel without
   knowledge?"
   Therefore I have declared what I did not understand,
   things too wonderful for me, which I did not know.

⁴ 'Hear, please, and I myself will speak;
   You said, "I will ask you, and you make it
   known to me".

⁵ 'I had heard of you by the hearing of the ear,
   but now my eye sees you.

⁶ 'Therefore I despise myself
   and repent in dust and ashes'.

Yahweh Rebukes Job's Friends

⁷ After Yahweh had spoken these words to Job, Yahweh said to Eliphaz the Temanite, 'My anger burns against you and against your two friends, for you have not spoken

straight to me as my servant Job has.[a]

8 'And now, take for yourselves seven bulls and seven rams, and go to my servant Job, and offer up for yourselves a burnt offering; and my servant Job will pray for you, because I will accept him so that I may not deal with you according to your folly, because you have not spoken straight to me like my servant Job'.

9 Then Eliphaz the Temanite, and Bildad the Shuhite, and Zophar the Naamathite went and did as Yahweh had commanded them; and Yahweh accepted Job.

Yahweh Restores Job's Fortunes

10 And Yahweh restored the fortunes[b] of Job when he prayed for his friends, and Yahweh increased all that Job had twofold.

11 Then all of his brothers, and all his sisters, and all of those who had known him before, came to Job. They ate bread with him in his house, and they consoled him and comforted him for all the adversity that Yahweh had brought upon him. Each one also gave him a piece of money and each an earring of gold.

12 So Yahweh blessed the latter days of Job more than his beginning; and he had fourteen thousand sheep, six thousand camels, a thousand yoke of oxen, and a thousand female donkeys.

13 He had also seven sons and three daughters.

14 He named the first daughter Jemima, the second Kezia, and the third Keren-happuch.

---

[a] Regarding the translation *to me* as opposed to *about me*, as found in KJV, NIV, ESV, etc., see Rick D. Moore, 'Raw Prayer and Refined Theology: "You Have Not Spoken Straight to Me, as My Servant Job Has"', in *The Spirit and the Mind: Essays in Informed Pentecostalism* (Lanham, MD: University Press of America, 2000), pp. 35-48.

[b] Lit., *turned the captivity*.

15 In all the land there were no women as beautiful as Job's daughters, and their father gave them an inheritance along with their brothers.[a]

16 After this, Job lived one hundred forty years, and he saw his sons and his sons' sons, four generations.

17 And Job died, old and full of days.

---

[a] See a similar situation, reported in Num. 27.1-7, where the daughters of Zelophehad were given an inheritance.

www.ingramcontent.com/pod-product-compliance
Lightning Source LLC
Chambersburg PA
CBHW052137090426
42741CB00009B/2122